WHAT IS YOUR WILL, O GOD?

JULES J. TONER, S.J.

WHAT IS YOUR WILL, O GOD?

*A Casebook for Studying
Discernment of God's Will*

THE INSTITUTE OF JESUIT SOURCES
1995

Number 12 in Series 4: Original Studies Composed in English

© The Institute of Jesuit Sources
3700 West Pine Boulevard
Saint Louis MO 63108
Tel: [314] 633-4622
Fax: [314] 633-4623
e-mail: ijs@jesuitsources.com

Library of Congress Catalogue Card Number 95-80588
ISBN 1-880810-14-x

CONTENTS

1. Introduction 1

2. Summary Statement of Ignatian Teaching
   on Discernment of God's Will 5

3. A Model of Discerning God's Will
   by Ignatius Himself 25

4. Cases with Questions for Reflection 33

5. Proposed Responses to the Questions for Reflection . . 79

✤   ONE   ✤

INTRODUCTION

The Purpose of This Book

An earlier book of mine, *Discerning God's Will*, was written to establish and clarify the teaching of St. Ignatius of Loyola on seeking and finding God's will. While depending on that earlier book, this book is more immediately practical: by applying Ignatius's teaching to concrete cases, it aims at helping students of discernment to develop or improve their skill in the Ignatian methods for seeking and finding God's will. My own experience over many years has convinced me that, apart from actually doing discernment under the personal direction of someone who has learning and skill, the most effective way of achieving or improving skill for doing or directing discernment of God's will is careful and sustained casework, especially when done with other serious students. In fact, such casework is sometimes, in some ways, even more effective than working with a skilled director. I have found this to be true for myself and for the many others with whom I have been associated in theology courses and workshops on individual and group discernment of God's will. Along with improving our skill in applying Ignatian teaching, casework serves also to make our understanding of that teaching more exact and penetrating.

In order to evaluate what is offered in this book and to use it most effectively, the reader must keep in mind its limited purpose. Although discernment of God's will, along with discernment of spirits, is essential to and fundamentally important in spiritual direction, the latter includes other important matters. Two conclusions follow. First, no one should be disappointed because these other matters are not treated here. Second, effective study of discerning God's will requires, especially at the beginning, a very concentrated effort. If when studying the cases on discerning God's will, readers allow their attention to be drawn away from questions regarding such discernment to other matters also involved in spiritual direction, however profitable these may be, they will be distracted from learning how to discern God's will and their progress will be retarded. I have often seen this happen. After developing some sound understanding of and skill in using Ignatian discernment of spirits and of God's will, students can more successfully achieve the integration of these with all else involved in spiritual direction than if they tried to do the integrating before having a sound foundation in discernment.

Presuppositions for Learning Ignatian Discernment of God's Will

Satisfactory use of this book presupposes an understanding of Ignatian teaching on discernment of spirits, at least a clear and firm grasp of the fundamentals. This understanding is needed to some degree for most discernment of God's will, but it is necessary in particular for what Ignatius calls the second mode of election (that is, in contemporary usage, of discerning God's will). This second mode of election cannot be carried out unless one possesses the ability to do discernment of spirits. For that reason, anyone who is not yet knowledgeable regarding Ignatian teaching on discernment of spirits would do well to study the latter before trying to use this book.[1]

The Cases: Sources and Kinds

Most cases presented in this book are accounts of actual experiences narrated firsthand or stories of another's experience as told by one who helped her or him through the discernment. As much as the aim of this book allows, these stories have been preserved in the narrator's own words. Some deletions or slight additions or adaptations have been made for the sake of clarity and precision, though sometimes ambiguities are deliberately left for the reader to deal with when answering the questions on that case. I have added the paragraph numbers to facilitate references to the case in the questions for reflection and in the responses to these.

It was not my intention that a preponderance of cases should deal with God's call to a state of life; but the cases which others presented or which I found in print led to this result. And, it must be said, it is these cases that Ignatius had primarily in mind when drawing up his directives for seeking God's will. If one learns to apply his teaching

---

[1] To help in that study, I have published two earlier volumes: *A Commentary on St. Ignatius' Rules for Discernment of Spirits* (St. Louis: The Institute of Jesuit Sources, 1981) and a casebook entitled *Spirit of Light or Darkness?* (St. Louis: The Institute of Jesuit Sources, 1995).

to this primary kind of case for discernment, there should be no problem in applying it to other types of cases. Besides, this book features enough of the other types of cases to give the reader a good start in doing so.

Nevertheless, I must admit that some important kinds of situations for discerning God's will do not appear at all among the cases in this book. This I regret. However, supplying all the types of cases in which students would be interested is not one of my concerns. What does concern me is to have cases in which all the main features of Ignatian teaching on discerning God's will are brought into play. If I have succeeded in doing that, then those who learn how to apply the essentials of Ignatian teaching to the cases presented here will be able to do the same to a variety of other cases. Rather than attempting to supply a paradigm case for every type of issue involving a discernment of God's will, I aim to help students develop a skill that will enable them to deal intelligently with any such issue.

Study Aids: Questions for Reflection, Reading, and Proposed Responses

After each case there are questions for reflection. The function of these is to keep the readers' attention and effort focused on some definite and significant matters in the case, to stimulate the readers to do some serious thinking, and to help them become aware of their present knowledge or ignorance, ability or inability to do discernment. These questions are not meant to cover everything of interest in the case; readers may think of further questions, whether of immediate relevance to discernment or to the wider scope of spiritual direction. It is wiser to save the latter kind of questions for consideration at a time when they will not interfere with concentration on discernment.

The questions for reflection and my proposed responses to them are couched in terms of Ignatian teaching. Now, what one thinks to be Ignatius's teaching depends on how one interprets what Ignatius has written. There are different interpretations of Ignatius's writing on the ways of seeking to find God's will.[2] The interpretation that shapes the questions and responses in this book can be found in my two earlier books, *A Commentary on St. Ignatius' Rules for Discernment of Spirits* and *Discerning God's Will.* For the benefit of those who are not familiar with *Discerning God's Will,* I have included in this book a highly con-

---

[2] See Jules Toner, S.J., *Discerning God's Will* (St. Louis: The Institute of Jesuit Sources, 1991), 5–8.

densed statement of the main conclusions in that earlier study, leaving aside the scholarship necessary to establish my interpretation of Ignatian writing on discernment, as well as a discussion of associated controversies.

The condensed statement is entitled "Summary Statement of Ignatian Teaching on Discernment of God's Will." On the basis of the experience of students, I can say that this statement has proved to be adequate for the purpose of working the cases in this book. However, those who studied *Discerning God's Will* in its entirety have found the complete text very much more helpful. With that in mind, I have inserted after the questions for reflection following each case references to appropriate pages in that book. The "Statement," however, is brief enough and, I hope, so coherently ordered and furnished with subheadings that after seriously studying these pages before taking up the cases, the reader can readily find the passages relevant for answering the questions for reflection.

TWO

Summary Statement of Ignatian Teaching on Discernment of God's Will

God's Will as Object of Ignatian Discernment

God's will as object of Ignatian discernment is God's positive, as distinct from his merely permissive, will. God wills to permit things that he would not positively will, for example, sin and the consequences of sin; his positive will, Ignatius holds as certain, is always what will be for his greater glory in us, for our ultimate greater happiness.

Among the things that God wills positively, some he wills with an effective, necessitating will. Such things happen independently of our free choice; they are beyond our control. God's will understood in this sense we can know only by prophecy or after the event. This will is entirely outside the scope of our discernment, which seeks to find what God wills before the event. We can choose to accept it lovingly and trustingly, or we can choose to respond negatively. Ultimately, however, God's effective, necessitating will is not something that we choose to do or not to do.

Some things that God wills positively he leaves to our free choice; concerning these, God has a preferential but non-necessitating will. We can freely choose to do what God prefers or to act otherwise. In these matters about which we have a free choice, Ignatian discernment is concerned only with God's positive preferential but non-necessitating will regarding the free choice made by an *individual* (or by a particular group) in some *concrete* situation. This individual is not concerned with finding God's universal will, for example, the principles of moral theology.

Among concrete situations about which God has a preferential will but allows the individual to exercise free choice, not every one of them lies within the compass of God's will as object of Ignatian discernment. Ignatius sees two different areas for discerning God's preferential will regarding individual free choices. In one, the discerner is trying to determine whether a proposed alternative for choice is morally permissible or is forbidden. In the other area, he or she already knows that every alternative for this choice is morally permissible in itself, but is trying to discern which one is, in this concrete situation, more for the glory of God in us. Ignatius's methods of discerning God's will are concerned solely with God's preferential will in this latter area.

From here on, unless the context makes clear that "God's will" is being used in some other meaning, this expression should be understood in this limited sense: God's positive, preferential but non-necessitating will regarding a person's free choice in a concrete situation when none of the alternatives for choice is commanded or forbidden by God. There are further limitations on the meaning of God's will as object of Ignatian discernment, but these cannot be satisfactorily treated before understanding our relationship with God in discerning his will. These further limitations will come up when studying cases and are best considered in that context.

Our Relationship with God in Discerning His Will

Understanding our relationship with God in discerning his will is a key to understanding all the rest of Ignatian teaching on this matter.

This teaching has to be understood within the context of the Ignatian Spiritual Exercises. An individual's relationship with God in making the Spiritual Exercises is a one-to-one, personal relationship of loving communion: God loving the person, communicating with him, and leading him to find what God wills; the person listening and responding to God, desiring to grow in love for him, and to know what God wants him to choose to do for God's greater glory.

The relationship is also a relationship of dependence and collaboration. We depend utterly on the guidance of the Holy Spirit to come to know God's will. We can guess (intelligently or stupidly) about what God wills, but we can have no justifiable faith that we have found God's will unless we also have a justifiable faith that the Holy Spirit has led us to our conclusion. This is so because the evidence we can gather for what God wills (in the limited meaning stated above) can justify only some probability, some reasonable guess. If we are to reach a faith conviction, we must have a justifiable belief that we have been led to our conclusion by the Holy Spirit. On the other hand, if we can be justifiably confident that the Holy Spirit has led us, we can be justifiably confident of having found God's will; the Holy Spirit will lead us only to the truth. However, Ignatius expects the Holy Spirit to lead us ordinarily only through the acts of our own minds and hearts, as we actively seek to find God's will. In other words, God's action in discernment does not replace human effort: he guides our seeking but does not substitute for it. He calls us to work with him in finding God's will for our lives of building his kingdom just as much as he calls us to work with him in carrying out in our lives the activities by which we try to build it.

THE ESSENTIAL CONDITIONS FOR SOUND DISCERNMENT OF GOD'S WILL

From the two basic truths about our relationship of dependence on and collaboration with the Holy Spirit in discerning God's will follow two essential conditions for sound discernment. From the first truth, our dependence on the Holy Spirit's guidance, we derive the first essential condition: Anyone seeking God's will must be open to the Holy Spirit. From the second truth, that the Holy Spirit ordinarily guides us through our own efforts, the second essential condition follows: We must carry out as best we can the search for God's will.

In order to have any justifiable belief that we are being led by the Holy Spirit in seeking God's will, we must be sure we are fulfilling these two conditions. It is, then, critically important to understand what this involves. Let us try to reach a thorough practical understanding of each of these conditions.

The First Essential Condition: Openness to the Holy Spirit

Of the two essential conditions for our discerning God's will, the first one, openness to the Spirit, is more important. In fact, nothing in the whole process of seeking God's will does more to assure success in this search.

Faith, charity, and hope, along with the humility that is prerequisite to and consequent on these, fundamentally constitute openness to the Holy Spirit in Christian life in general. Within the particular context of discerning God's will, certain particular expressions of faith, hope, and charity in a Christian life open to the Holy Spirit need to be stressed. The first is a sincere intention to do whatever God wills, no matter what the cost. Seeking to know God's will with the intention that, once we have learned what it is, we will then deliberate whether or not to do it, is worse than a waste of time. The second element to be stressed is an intense and persevering desire and petition to know God's will, accompanied by faith that God will lead me to know it. The third element is indifference to every alternative for choice except insofar as it seems to be God's will.

This indifference is the essential condition that is hardest to attain and easiest to overlook. For this reason Ignatius in his instructions on seeking God's will never tires of recalling and emphasizing this quality (*Spiritual Exercises,* ¶¶1, 5, 16, 23, 146, 147, 155–57, 166, 169, 179, 184, 189). It is, as we shall see, the sure expression of and test of faith, hope, and charity, the ultimate criterion of openness to the Holy Spirit; and, more than anything else, therefore, it is the key to successful discernment of God's will. All the meditation or contemplation and self-examination in the Spiritual Exercises prior to the Election is directed toward achieving it. Understanding it is fundamental if we are to have any comprehension of Ignatian discernment. So at this point let us look more deeply into indifference.

In general, apart from its special meaning in the context of Ignatian discernment, indifference entails an affective attitude that is a mean between contrary affects such as love and hate, desire and aversion, hope and fear, joy and sorrow; it negates each of these contraries. Commentators frequently understand indifference as a state of affective apathy toward some person, event, or thing; but this interpretation might be questionable even in general. Indeed, in the context of Ignatian discernment of God's will, as we shall see, such an understanding would be all wrong.

When the term "indifference" is used in the context of discerning God's will, it denotes indifference to every alternative for choice prior to deciding which one God prefers, which one is more for God's glory in us. The contribution that indifference makes to discernment is that it frees one to see the truth by preventing any spontaneous attraction to or aversion from an alternative that might influence the judgment. It is not sufficient that discerners are so free that when they see what God wills, they will choose it; that degree of freedom may still leave discerners unwittingly blinded by their desires and fears. When adequately indifferent, discerners are so immune from the influence of selfish desires for or fears of any alternatives that they are not only entirely ready to choose whatever they find as God's will but also so free that no desire or fear will influence their discernment processes, will be the father of their thought. No one lacking such freedom is ready to undertake discernment.

When truly indifferent, the will of the discerner regarding the alternatives for choice is like a balance at equilibrium, ready to be weighed down on either side by the evidence for what God wills. Another, perhaps a deeper, way of putting it is that those persons who have reached indifference to all but God's will have already made their choice in principle; that is to say, they have already chosen whatever will turn out to be God's will. At the moment of finalized judgment, the choice in principle becomes ipso facto an actual choice specified by that judgment. The problem in discerning God's will should never be whether discerners will choose to do what they judge to be God's will; it should be only an intellectual problem of reaching a sound judgment.

Although this attitude of indifference is not easy to attain, we must not represent it as harder than it is. It does not necessarily involve freedom from all attraction to or aversion from alternatives (sometimes it should not or cannot), but only freedom from the power of these to sway the discerner's judgment. The gap between the power of these attractions and aversions and the power of discerners' greater desire to know and do God's will is the measure of their indifference. It is adequate when the desire to know and do God's will is so much greater than other desires that the latter are rendered impotent to determine the discerners' judgment of what God wills.

If we understand what the attitude of indifference is in the context of discerning God's will and also what underlying affective response makes it possible, we will clearly perceive that regarding indifference as apathy is far from Ignatius's meaning and could result in harmful consequences. First of all, indifference itself is an affective *response* that views each alternative for choice as unworthy of being chosen over the other unless it is seen to be more for God's glory. Further, indifference depends on an intense affective response of desire to know and do what is more for the kingdom of God. This desire, in turn, depends on an intense love for God and neighbor. So intense is this love and desire in those who are adequately indifferent for discerning God's will that no love or desire unrelated to love for God and desire for his kingdom can influence their judgment.

Why then stress the negative aspect of this response to God by emphasizing indifference? Why not speak only of love for God and of desire for God's glory? Another question can suggest the answer to this question: Why did Jesus say, "If anyone will follow me, let him deny himself and take up his cross and follow me"? Why didn't he say more positively, "If anyone will follow me let him love me and desire God's kingdom above all else"? The answers to this question and to the one raised about indifference are the same. The test of our love for God and our desire to bring about the kingdom of God is how much we are willing to give up and endure. It is so easy to have delightful feelings of love and to think we are very unselfish when, in fact, our love for God or neighbor is weak and shot through with self-seeking. Our readiness or unreadiness to let go of self-centered desires, to endure loss and pain, is a sure test of how pure and strong our love for God and desire for the kingdom of God really are.

The Second Essential Condition for Sound Discernment of God's Will

The second essential condition, we saw above, requires that the discerner make every reasonable effort to find God's will, to carry through the process of seeking for it. What does this involve? First, it involves trying to find the most helpful methods of seeking for God's will. Second, it involves learning how to use these methods by study, by gaining experience in using them under direction, and by reflection on our experience. Ignatius himself worked for years in perfecting the Spiritual Exercises as a way for an individual to seek God's will.

TIMES FOR AND MODES OF DISCERNING GOD'S WILL

The Holy Spirit can, of course, give supernaturally infused clarity and certainty of what God wills us to choose in any concrete situation; but, as we stated above, we have no reason to expect such an extraordinary event. We should expect the Spirit to guide us through the workings of our own minds and hearts. Now, whenever with our human reason we try to reach a sound decision, we have to gather the evidence for each alternative, weigh the opposing sets of evidence, and so come to a conclusion.

Ignatius sees three kinds of data from which we can extract three kinds of evidence for what God wills us to choose. He sees three corresponding times or occasions at which each kind of data is given in spiritual experiences or sought by rational investigation. To correspond with these three times or occasions, Ignatius presents three modes of discerning God's will. We will refer to these as the first, second, and third modes or the first-time, second-time, and third-time modes.

For historical accuracy it should be noted that Ignatius did not himself speak as we do of times for and modes of *discerning* God's will, but of times for and modes of *election* or of seeking and finding God's will. Without going into refinements, we can say that for our purposes the several terms can be taken as equivalent. (See the table on page 12.)

The First Time for and the First Mode of Seeking God's Will

The first mode of seeking God's will begins with a spiritual experience given by God, one not attainable by any human effort, an experience we will refer to as a first-time experience. Without this experience, which we cannot induce in ourselves, the first mode of discerning God's will is impossible. "The first is a time when God our Lord so moves and draws the will that, without doubting or the power of doubting, the faithful person follows what is shown, as St. Paul and St. Matthew did in following of Christ our Lord" (*Sp. Ex.*, ¶175).

There are three essential factors in this experience:

1. First, Ignatius speaks of a movement of the will, that is, a volitional tendency towards something to be done, a conative act of will (not a feeling of consolation in the affective sensibility; not a word is said about spiritual consolation).

2. Next, Ignatius speaks of "what is shown." In context, the phrase clearly means that to which the will is moved as to what God wills.

3. Finally, there is a twofold certitude: It is impossible for the person who has a first-time experience to doubt either that the movement is from God or that what is shown is what God wills.

Does the person having a first-time experience know God's will without further ado? Some think that that is the case. If so, then it seems that what we have called the first-time mode of discerning God's will is not a mode of discerning at all, at least not in any active sense of discerning. In this matter, however, there is sound reason to entertain a different opinion. It is true that no reflection seems to be needed in order to have a spontaneously certain judgment of what God wills. But is that enough for the subject of the experience to fulfill the second essential condition for reaching a trustworthy judgment about God's will? Should the person not reflectively verify the experience and reach a reflectively validated certitude? In other words, I am suggesting, the first-time experience, even with its spontaneous certainty of what God wills, is only data for a discernment by critical reflection on it. By such reflection, the person who has the experience can arrive at a critically validated reflective certainty or a critically justified doubt about the unreflective certainty.

Schema for Comparing and Contrasting the Ignatian Times for and Modes of Discerning God's Will (of "election")

	Time for discerning God's Will	Data	Discernment process
The *first* mode of discerning God's will	When a first-time experience is given	The first-time experience	1. Critical evaluation of the data to see whether it was a genuine first-time experience 2. If genuine, then assent with reflective certainty of what was shown as God's will in the direct experience
The *second* mode of discerning God's will	When second-time experiences are given	The second-time experience	1. Critical evaluation of the data to see whether the consolations and desolations were spiritual; if so, whether they were prompted by the Holy Spirit or the evil spirit; if by the Holy Spirit, whether they were integral with the attraction to one of the alternatives for choice 2. Interpretation of the evaluated data to get evidence by applying the pertinent rules for discernment of spirits 3. Weighing evidence and concluding tentatively 4. Seeing confirmation and finalizing the conclusion
The *third* mode of discerning God's will	When the discerner is in a "tranquil time"	Relevant information necessary for a trustworthy deliberation on the likely consequences of each alternative for the service and glory of God	1. Critical evaluation of the data 2. Interpretation of the evaluated data to get evidence, by applying the *magis* principle (see *Sp. Ex.*, ¶¶178–83) 3. Weighing the evidence and concluding tentatively 4. Seeking confirmation and finalizing the conclusion

To that end a number of questions have to be answered. Is "what is shown" in accord with Holy Scripture, with the Church's teaching, and with sound reason? Is it accurately grasped and remembered, nothing added to or taken away from it, no interpretation imposed on it by the person's own presupposition? Is it indubitable? Or can the recipient doubt it if he or she tries to do so? Does applying the basic rules for discernment of spirits bring to the fore any questionable factor regarding its origin? Was the judgment of what God wills immediately given by the movement of the will toward some choice, or is it the conclusion of an immediate inference (so easy and so rapid as to seem like an intuition) and, therefore, really a discernment in the third mode? Or was there an intuition that in no way depended on a movement of the will by God? There are so many ways that mistakes could creep in here that failure to do serious reflection on the experience would seem to be grave negligence in fulfilling the second essential condition for seeking God's will.

The Second Time for and Mode of Discerning God's Will

The second mode of seeking God's will also begins from a spiritual experience, one given in the second time. This is "a time when light and understanding are gathered plentifully through experiences of consolations and desolations and through experience of discerning diverse spirits" (*Sp. Ex.,* ¶176).

Discernment of God's will in the second mode (a second-time discernment) has three main steps. First, the discerner must have the kind of spiritual experiences to which we will refer as second-time experiences. These are primarily movements of the Holy Spirit; in a secondary way, antispiritual movements can also be of some use in this mode of discernment and can be called second-time experiences. Until second-time movements are experienced, the second mode of discerning God's will is not possible. When they are experienced, a time or occasion for making a second-time discernment has arrived. The unreflected second-time experiences are not themselves evidence of God's will, but only data for reflection. The second step, therefore, in this mode of discernment is methodical reflection on these data in order to find evidence and arrive at a decision. The decision reached is at first only tentative; the discerner is to seek confirmation of it before finalizing it.

Seeking confirmation is the third step. Let us see what is involved in each of these main steps.[1]

Any second-time experience has two essential and related factors. First, there is a conative movement of will, a volitional attraction, toward one of the alternatives for choice. Discerners do not experience attraction to this alternative because in itself it appeals more to them, because they like it; rather, they are drawn to it as to what God wills them to choose. Whether for any other reason or motive they like it or dislike it is irrelevant in this mode of discernment. The motivation for the attraction, in other words, is pure or, as Ignatius would say, "from above." This movement is similar to the movement of will in the first-time experience, but not as powerful as the latter and without the certainty about the divine source of it that accompanies the latter.

Second, such a volitional movement, then, needs some further factor as a sign that the movement arises at the prompting of the Holy Spirit and not from some antispiritual or nonspiritual source. Ignatius looks for this sign in spiritual consolation. So also, movements of spiritual desolation are signs of the influence of the evil spirit. What characterizes spiritual consolation and desolation and why these are signs of the influence of the Holy Spirit or of the evil spirit are questions taken up in Ignatius's rules for discernment of spirits.

It is not enough, however, that the spiritual consolation or desolation comes only before or only after the experienced drawing of the will, even immediately before or after. It must be present during the drawing, the attraction. What is more, it is not even enough that the two factors are experienced simultaneously; they must be so integrated that one is the matrix from within which the other arises, and the two form a single experience.

Reflection on the Second-Time Experiences

This step is to be carried out when the spiritual movements have subsided, when the discerner is spiritually calm and also free from any nonspiritual hindrances to clear recall and critical thought, for instance, excessive tiredness, emotional disturbance, distraction.

---

[1] The second-time experiences, as we shall see, involve as an essential factor movements of spiritual consolation or desolation. Without a clear and accurate understanding of these movements, described in Ignatius's rules for discernment of spirits, as also of other teachings in those rules, the second mode of discernment cannot be correctly understood. That is why study of Ignatian discernment of spirits should precede study of his teaching on discernment of God's will.

The reflective step in second-time discernment of God's will has three main parts or stages: (1) critical evaluation of each second-time experience, (2) interpretation of the experiences critically evaluated in order to derive evidence regarding God's will, and (3) weighing evidence and reaching a tentative conclusion. Each part or stage needs some explanation. The following discussion will be limited to those second-time experiences that include spiritual consolation; whatever needs to be said about experiences with spiritual desolation can be added briefly afterwards.

What is involved in critical evaluation of second-time experiences can be shown in an ordered series of questions.

1. Is the object of volitional attraction, what appeared in the experience as God's will, accurately recalled, without addition or subtraction? After or even at the time of the experience, we can impose some meaning of our own, either a meaning we want to find in it or a meaning that rests on some assumption. On the other hand, we can sift out something contained in it that we do not want to hear.

2. Is that object of volition in accord with Sacred Scripture, Church teaching, and sound reason?

3. Is the motivation for it pure, that is, does it spring from love for God entirely or mainly? Or does it derive from our self-love with its consequent self-centered desires and aversions, hopes and fears?

4. Is the volitional attraction not only simultaneous but also integral with the spiritual consolation or merely an accompaniment of it?

5. Is the consolation truly spiritual, that is, rooted in spiritual faith, hope, and love?

6. If the consolation is truly spiritual, is it prompted by the Holy Spirit, not by the evil spirit acting "as an angel of light"?

Unless *all* the above questions are answered affirmatively, there is no point in proceeding to any further step in reflection, for the experience cannot be evidence for what God wills.

If the questions are all answered affirmatively, then the time has come to interpret the critically evaluated data in order to get evidence for what is God's will. If the consolation is spiritual and integral with the volitional impulse and from the Holy Spirit, this experience offers some probable evidence that God wills the object of the volitional impulse. Why that is so should be clear to those who understand Ignatian discernment of spirits. Once discerners are familiar with discernment of spirits, they find that interpreting second-time experiences to discover evidence is an easy step in comparison to the previous step of critical evaluation.

When the second-time experience is a volitional attraction or aversion with desolation, that experience must also be critically evaluated. Is the desolation truly spiritual (in the sense of antispiritual)? That is, does it directly attack faith, hope, and charity? Is it integral with the drawing? If the answers to these questions indicate that the desolation is not spiritual or not integral with the volitional drawing, then the whole experience is useless for second-time discernment of God's will. If the desolation is spiritual and is integral with volitional attraction, then the experience is to be interpreted in a way contrary to a second-time experience with spiritual consolation. In other words, the experience is contraindicative of God's will: it is one bit of evidence that the subject is being drawn to something that is not God's will.

The third part of the reflective step in second-time discernment is weighing evidence and coming to a tentative conclusion. One must ask such questions as the following. Is the evidence significantly weightier on one side than on the other? Is it weighty enough to justify coming to a decision? But when is there enough evidence? Ignatius says that in this kind of discernment process we need "much light," not just one or two significant experiences or a number of trivial ones. When the evidence can be called sufficient is, of course, a matter of judgment, and nothing can take the place of sound judgment. Some helpful signs that one has enough evidence can be found in Ignatius's account of his own discernment. One sign is the sense of assurance that the discerner has done all that can reasonably be done to search out God's will. Another is the sense of security, of freedom from fear that one might be making a decision that is in discord with God's will.

A word of caution regarding this mode of discernment seems called for. Given the subtleties and difficulties of the second mode of discernment, discerners seem to be acting unwisely and failing to fulfill the second essential condition for sound discernment when they undertake it without having adequate skill based on learning and experience in discerning spirits and in doing this mode of discerning God's will—unless they do so under the direction of someone who has such skill. Even when one is equipped for this mode of discernment, as we shall see, it seems wise to combine it with the third mode of discerning God's will.

The Third Time for and Mode of Seeking God's Will

In the *Spiritual Exercises* Ignatius gives a much fuller treatment to the third time for and mode of seeking God's will than he does to the first and second. He notes there what he calls two ways or methods, but when we analyze them they appear as one way. For the so-called second way is merely a series of four "rules" that can serve as helps to purify and intensify the attitudes essential for successful discernment when the seeker of God's will is not finding it by this third-time mode of seeking. All these "rules" are calculated to help purify and intensify the discerners' love and desire, rendering them more fully indifferent to all but God's will and stronger in their longing for knowledge of that will. In fact, these rules could all be followed to advantage in any preparation for discerning God's will. They are not, apart from the "first way," methods of getting and interpreting data so as to find third-time evidence.

Here is Ignatius's statement of the third time for and the first, the basic, way of proceeding in the third mode:

The third is a tranquil time, when one considers, first what a person is born for, that is, to praise God our Lord and to save his soul; and when, desiring to do this, the person elects as a means to help serve God and save his soul a way or state of life within the boundaries of the Church. I said a tranquil time, a time when the person is not stirred up by diverse spirits and has free and tranquil use of his natural powers.

If an election is not made in the first or the second time, there follow two ways of making it which belong to this third time.

THE FIRST WAY [IN THIS THIRD TIME] TO MAKE A SOUND AND TRUSTWORTHY ELECTION CONTAINS SIX POINTS

The first point is to put before my mind the question about which I wish to make an election, for instance, whether to accept or refuse an office or a benefice, or anything else that is a matter for a changeable election. [That is to say, it is not something which the person cannot change by a legitimate choice.]

The second point. It is necessary to have as my goal the end for which I am created, which is to praise God our Lord and to save my soul. Along with that, it is necessary that I have become indifferent about any disordered affections, so that I am neither more inclined or affected toward taking than leaving what is proposed [for election] nor more inclined toward leaving than taking it. Rather, it is necessary that I find myself like a balance at midpoint, in order to pursue whatever I perceive to be more for the glory and praise of God our Lord and the salvation of my soul.

The third point is to beg God our Lord that he be pleased to move my will and to put in me what I ought to do about the matter proposed. That is, what may be more to his praise and glory. Then with my understanding I should well and faithfully range back and forth [in search of reasons or in reflection on them] and make a choice conformed to his most holy and agreeable will.

The fourth point is to investigate with reasoned arguments how many advantages or gains solely for the praise of God our Lord and the salvation of my soul will accrue to me from having the proposed office or benefice [or whatever else is proposed for choice]; and, on the contrary, to make a parallel investigation of the disadvantages and perils from having it. Then, the second step will be to go through the same process for the other alternative, that is, to examine the advantages and gains of having it and, likewise, on the contrary, the disadvantages and perils of not having it.

The fifth point. After going back and forth [over the advantages and disadvantages] in this way and having reasoned on the matter [for election] from all sides, to observe toward which alternative reason leans. In this way, the decision on the matter proposed ought to be reached in accord with what sways reason more powerfully and not in accord with what moves sensuality.

The sixth point. After such an election or decision, the person who has made it ought to go to prayer before God our Lord with great diligence and offer him the said election so that His Divine Majesty may be pleased to accept and confirm it, provided it be for his greater service and praise.

What Ignatius says about the third time for and mode of seeking to find God's will is not difficult to follow. Nevertheless, a few clarifications and a suggestion or two might help toward a more exact understanding of the foregoing passage.

The third time for discerning God's will is, St. Ignatius says, "a tranquil time." By that he means, first, a time when the discerners are not experiencing movements of the spirits, such as those that characterize the second time for election, or other movements (excitement, elation or depression, worry, and so on). He also means a time when one is free of other distractions, such as tiredness, pain, noise, and so on. In short, he means a time when the discerner is unimpeded by anything that would interfere with the "free and tranquil" exercise of reason and judgment.

During this tranquil time, the discerner is to gather information, formulate reasons (advantages and disadvantages for each alternative), list, organize, and comparatively weigh reasons for each side, and finally reach a decision. Several comments will be of practical value for doing this in a simpler and more orderly way.

1. To show only that an alternative is in some way for the service and glory of God is not a reason for thinking it is God's will. To be a reason for such a judgment, it must be shown that the alternative is in some respect *more* for God's service and glory

than the other alternative. That is what it means to speak of an advantage for one alternative.

2. No advantage or disadvantage found in one of the alternatives for choice has any significance for discerning God's will except insofar as it is, at least reductively, an advantage or disadvantage for the glory of God. Every other kind of advantage or disadvantage, no matter what, is irrelevant.

3. A disadvantage for one alternative is equivalent to an advantage for the other alternative.

4. Ordinarily, each alternative will, in some respect or respects, have an advantage for God's service over the other. There will, therefore, usually be evidence favoring each of the alternatives and a need to weigh the sets of evidence against each other.

5. This evidence for both sides can be more effectively found if the discerner takes the alternatives one at a time and strives to make the case as powerful as possible for each in turn.

6. Once the reasons are formulated and organized, the discerner should critically review them (time and again when the question is an important one), deleting those that on reflection are seen as invalid, correcting those that are ·in some way faulty, adding new reasons if these come to mind, noting which reasons are the strongest and deserve more consideration—doing all this prayerfully, patiently, and with alertness for any falling away from indifference to all but God's will.

The Distinction, Autonomy, and Combination of the Three Modes

In the preceding description of the three modes of discerning God's will, we can detect a common basic process. There is in each mode the following steps:

1. Receiving or searching out what appears to be relevant data
2. Critical evaluation of the data
3. Interpretation of the evaluated data to find evidence pro or con
4. Weighing of the evidence and drawing a conclusion

Nevertheless, we can also see that each of the three modes is fully distinct from the other two by reason of

1. different kinds of data
2. different principles for critically evaluating data

3. different principles for interpreting the critically evaluated data in order to derive evidence

4. different kinds of evidence derived from interpretation of the data

The three distinct modes, furthermore, are not merely distinct parts of a single complete and adequate way of finding God's will. Rather, each one can be autonomous; that is, each one can be by itself adequate for finding God's will, can function independently of the other two for reaching a trustworthy conclusion.

Nevertheless, whenever it is reasonably possible to do so, it seems better, more in accord with Ignatius's practice and with the explicit recommendation of the early directories for the Spiritual Exercises, to use more than one complete mode of discernment, especially to combine the second and third modes, testing each by the other. (This is not the same as seeking confirmation for the conclusion of one type of discernment by employing some sort of evidence peculiar to another. This will be made clearer in the following section on confirmation.) In fact, when it is reasonably possible to do so, it even seems requisite to combine the second and third modes in order to fulfill the second essential condition for sound discernment, that is, that we must make every reasonable effort. If our effort is less than our reasonable best, we have reason to doubt that the Holy Spirit has guided us to our conclusion.

Seeking Confirmation (or Disconfirmation) of the Tentative Decision

In his instructions on the method of carrying out a discernment in the third mode, Ignatius advises discerners to bring their tentative decision to God for confirmation (or disconfirmation) before finalizing them and putting them into execution. Neither in the *Spiritual Exercises* nor in the *Autograph Directory*, however, does Ignatius say anything about seeking confirmation for the conclusion of a second-time discernment. These considerations have led many commentators to think that there is no need to seek confirmation before finalizing and beginning to execute a decision reached by the second mode of discernment, and that second-time experiences alone constitute the confirmation sought for a decision by the third mode (even though Ignatius himself never explicitly says either of these things). A third idea, constantly put forward by those commentators who think that Ignatius saw little or no value in the third mode of election by itself, holds that seeking confirmation in the third mode is equivalent to moving into a second-time election. Apart from the second mode, they say, the third mode of discernment is useless for finding God's will, at least in any important matter.

It is impossible here to summon up all the textual evidence showing that every one of these three opinions is at variance with Ignatius's teaching and practice. (I have done this in *Discerning God's Will*, 201f.) At present I shall have to content myself with proposing my own interpretation of what Ignatius means by confirmation to be sought at the end of an election and what kind of experiences can constitute confirmation; then I shall answer several further questions about the process of seeking confirmation.

Meaning of Confirmation

To grasp the meaning of confirmation in the context of Ignatian discernment, we must distinguish confirmation of the will to carry out the decision (volitional confirmation) from confirmation of the decision about, the judgment of, what is God's will (intellectual confirmation). It is principally confirmation in the second meaning that Ignatius wants the discerner to seek before finalizing a decision. It is obvious in Ignatius's *Spiritual Journal* that he sought confirmation in this meaning not only for a third-time decision but also when his second-time discernment led powerfully to a conclusion.

What, then, constitutes confirmation in this meaning? On the basis of the account Ignatius gives in his *Spiritual Journal* (and on what seems to be soundly in accord with good sense and the experience of good Christians), there are a number of different forms of confirmation for the tentative conclusion of a discernment.

1. Second-time experiences can confirm a decision in the third mode of discernment, or added experiences of this kind can confirm a decision by the second mode.

2. More intense attraction toward what is tentatively judged to be God's will, because it is God's will, even without spiritual consolation, can be a confirmation for the conclusion of either mode of discernment.

3. Reasons, in the sense of third-time evidence, can confirm a tentative decision reached by second-time evidence. A decision reached by third-time evidence can be confirmed by new evidence of the same kind or by seeing greater force in the evidence by which the tentative decision was reached.

4. An increased sense of certainty, of security in having found God's will, even without spiritual consolation, can confirm the tentative decision reached by any kind of evidence.

5. So also, being freed from fear of the painful consequences of carrying out the decision can confirm the truth of the decision resulting from any mode of discernment. (When this happens, we have a volitional confirmation serving *also* as an intellectual confirmation.)

6. It even seems possible to have a decision confirmed by a quasi first-time experience. (I have come across at least one clear case.)

In relation to what we said above about combining modes of discernment, it is important to distinguish between testing a discernment by another complete discernment in a different mode and confirming it by some kind of evidence peculiar to that other mode. Ignatius's practice, as described in his *Spiritual Journal*, shows that he did make a clear distinction between combining the second and third modes of seeking God's will and searching for confirmation of the conclusion by the kind of evidence peculiar to each of these modes. He reached the same tentative conclusion resoundingly in complete and distinct discernments by both methods and afterwards sought and found confirmation for that common conclusion in the ways noted above (1–4). Even apart from Ignatius's practice, the distinction between using an added complete mode of discernment and seeking confirmation by some evidence of the kind used in that mode should be clear: What could be very satisfactory confirmation might be not at all sufficient for establishing the tentative conclusion to be confirmed.

Some Questions about the Way to Seek and the Necessity of Seeking and Receiving Confirmation

Several further questions need attention:

1. How does one go about seeking confirmation?

2. When is confirmation sufficient to justify finalizing a tentative decision?

3. Is seeking confirmation necessary for a sound discernment?

4. Is receiving confirmation before finalizing and executing the decision necessary for a sound discernment?

Just as with the preceding matters concerning confirmation, about the only source of light on these questions is Ignatius's own practices as recounted in his *Spiritual Journal*, along with what is said in the early directories.

1. The search for confirmation should proceed in much the same way as the search for evidence before the tentative decision. The discerner must be indifferent as to the outcome, ready to accept the necessity of further efforts to discern if God should delay confirmation or even disconfirm the conclusion. (This is a very difficult attitude to maintain; even Ignatius tells how on one occasion he became impatient with the Holy Trinity when he did not receive the strong confirmation he looked for.) So also a discerner must carry on in meditation and waiting on God with intense and persevering petition for light, with faith that God hears and will answer the petition. In these attitudes of indifference and prayer, the discerner is to repeatedly go over the evidence by which he has arrived at this conclusion, evaluating it, weighing it, taking it to God in prayer.

2. When is confirmation sufficient to justify finalizing the tentative decision and putting it into execution? The signs to be found in Ignatius's own practice seem to be these two: The discerner feels confident of having done all that is reasonable in seeking confirmation and has a sense of security in the decision reached, freedom from fear of going against God's will.

3. Is it necessary for sound discernment of God's will to seek confirmation? It is necessary if it is reasonable to do so in the situation, that is to say, if the discerner has the time and energy to do so and if the decision is important enough to warrant expenditure of that time and energy. Otherwise seeking confirmation is not necessary.

4. If confirmation is to be sought, is it necessary for a sound discernment actually to receive confirmation before finalizing the tentative decision? The answer is negative. If after all reasonable effort no significant confirmation or disconfirmation is given, discerners should finalize the decision and act on it, regarding the absence of disconfirmation as a tacit confirmation. For after discerners have sought God's will as best they can, with openness to the Spirit and with all reasonable effort, they can rightly think that the Holy Spirit in his loving providence will in some way lead them to the truth about what will be for the greater glory of God in us. Therefore, discerners can rightly judge that if the Holy Spirit disapproved of their decisions, he would in some way let this be known. The early directories for the *Spiritual Exercises* explicitly advise discerners to act on their decisions even when they receive no confirmation after having done their best to seek it.

✤ THREE ✤

A MODEL OF DISCERNING GOD'S WILL
BY IGNATIUS HIMSELF

F rom original sources we have some information on how Ignatius himself went about discerning God's will, but for only one of his discernments do we have a detailed account of the process. This one he made while composing the Constitutions for the newly founded Society of Jesus. The question for discernment had to do with some concrete issue about how Jesuits were to practice poverty. Without further elucidation, it will be enough for our purpose to say that it bore on observing poverty more or less strictly and completely. Our concern is only with the process.

There are two closely related documents which reveal that process. In one of these we have a carefully organized statement of the reasons, arrived at in the third mode of election, that support each of the alternatives for choice. The second document is a section of his spiritual journal or diary in which Ignatius relates mainly the spiritual experiences constituting evidence in the second mode of election, that is, spiritual consolations integral with attraction to one alternative. In the course of this account, however, he tells how time and again he spent long periods of critical reflection on the reasons, the third-time evidence, he had already drawn up; on occasion he also adds new reasons as these occur to him.

These two documents, in which we can see the master following his own teaching, not only illustrate his doctrine but also serve to answer a number of critically important questions that he does not answer in the *Spiritual Exercises* or elsewhere. Many of the questions for reflection on the cases in this book and much of what is said in the proposed responses to them depend on what is in these documents, especially the journal. For that reason, it seemed necessary to include them in this book.[1]

---

[1] Both documents are given in the English translation made by William J. Young, S.J., *The Spiritual Journal of St. Ignatius Loyola* (Woodstock, Md.:

25

[Ignatius's Election Process by the Third Mode]

The disadvantages in having no revenue are the advantages in having a partial or adequate revenue.

1. It seems that the Society will be better maintained if it has a partial or adequate revenue.

2. If the members have revenues they will avoid annoying or disedifying others, seeing that for the most part they will have to be clerics who do the begging.

3. Having a revenue they will avoid temptations to an ill-ordered solicitude in seeking support.

4. The Society will be able to give itself with greater order and peace of mind to offices and prayers at the appointed times.

5. The time that would be spent in soliciting could be given to preaching, hearing confessions, and other pious works.

6. It seems that the church in this way will be kept cleaner and better adorned, thus moving to devotion, and offering the possibility of rebuilding.

7. The members of the Society will thus be able to give themselves to study and by this means be of greater spiritual help to the neighbor, and care for their own health.

8. After two of the Society considered the matter, all the others approved of it.

The disadvantages in having a revenue are the advantages in not having any, namely:

1. With a revenue the members would not be so diligent in helping the neighbor, nor so ready to go on journeys and endure adversity. Moreover, they could not so well persuade the neighbor to true poverty and self-abnegation in all things, as is seen among the advantages of having no revenue, which follow:

Advantages and reasons for having no revenue.

1. The Society will have greater spiritual strength and greater devotion by a closer resemblance to the Son of the Virgin, our Creator and Lord, who lived in such great poverty and hardship.

2. By not looking for a definite income, all worldly greed will the more readily be put to flight.

3. Because it seems that the Society is thus united with greater love to the Church, if there is uniformity among the members in having nothing and if they look to the poverty of Christ in the Blessed Sacrament.

4. It will be easier to hope for everything from God our Lord if we thus withdraw from everything belonging to the world.

Woodstock College Press, 1958), 1–5, 61–63.

5. There will be greater help in humbling ourselves, and a greater union with Him who humbled Himself more than all.

6. The Society will live in greater disregard of all worldly consolation.

7. It will live continually in greater hope of God's help and with greater care in His service.

8. There will be in general greater edification, seeing that we seek nothing belonging to the world.

9. We can speak with greater liberty of spirit and greater effectiveness on all spiritual subjects to the greater profit of souls.

10. There will be greater help and encouragement to help souls when alms are received daily.

11. He will better persuade others to embrace true poverty who observes that which Christ our Lord recommended when He said, "If anyone has left father," etc.

12. It seems that we shall be more active in helping the neighbor and readier to go on journeys and endure hardships.

13. Poverty, without any income, is more perfect than poverty with a partial or adequate income.

14. In choosing this for Himself, Jesus, Lord of us all, taught it to His apostles and beloved disciples when He sent them to preach.

15. It was this that all ten of us unanimously chose when we took the same Jesus Christ our Creator and Lord as our leader, to go to preach and exhort under His standard, which is our vocation.

16. According to this understanding of poverty the Bull was issued at our petition, and after waiting a year for it to be expedited, while we persevered in the same understanding, it was confirmed by His Holiness.

17. It is an attribute of God our Lord to be unchangeable, and a quality of the enemy to be inconstant and changeable.

[Ignatius's Election Process by the Second Mode]

Our Lady.[2]

1. Saturday [February 2].—Deep devotion at Mass, with tears and increased confidence in Our Lady, and more inclination to complete poverty then and throughout the day.

2. Sunday [February 3].—The same, and more inclination to no revenue then and throughout the day.

---

[2] Before each day's notation describing what he had experienced regarding the election he was making, St. Ignatius indicated the liturgical formula for the Mass he had offered on that day, for example, the Mass in honor of the Trinity, the Name of Jesus, the Holy Spirit, our Lady.

Our Lady.

3. Monday [February 4].—The same, and with other feelings, and more inclined to no revenue throughout the day, and by night, a turning to Our Lady with deep affection and much confidence.

Our Lady.

4. Tuesday [February 5].—An abundance of devotion before Mass, during it, and after it, tears and eye-pains because of so many of them. I saw Mother and Son disposed to intercede with the Father, (V)[3] and felt more inclined to perfect poverty at the time and throughout the day; in the evening I knew or saw as it were that our Lady was inclined to intercede.

Our Lady.

5. Wednesday [February 6].—Devotion before Mass and during it, not without tears, more inclined to perfect poverty. Later I thought with sufficient clearness, or change from the ordinary, that there would be some confusion in having a partial revenue, and a scandal in having a complete revenue, and an occasion for making little of the poverty which our Lord praises so highly.

The Most Holy Trinity.

6. Thursday [February 7].—Before Mass with deep devotion and tears, and a notable warmth and devotion all through the day, being always moved more to perfect poverty. At the time of Mass, I thought there was a notable impulse with deep devotion and interior movement to ask the Father, as I thought my mediators had interceded for me, and I had some indication of seeing them.

The Name of Jesus.

7. Friday [February 8].—After notable devotion and tears at prayer, beginning with preparation for Mass, and during it with deep devotion and tears also, holding my tongue when I could, with the decision for perfect poverty.

Soon after Mass, with devotion and not without tears, going through the elections for an hour and a half or more and making an offering of what seemed to be better supported by reason, and by a stronger inclination of will, that is, to have no revenue, wishing to present this to the Father through the mediation [medio] and prayers of the Mother and the Son, I prayed first to her to help me with her Son and the Father, and then prayed to the Son to help me with His Father in company with the Mother[.] I felt within me an impulse to go and betake myself to the Father, and in doing so my hair stood on end, with a most remarkable warmth in my whole body. Following on this, tears and the deepest devotion (V).

---

[3] A sign made by St. Ignatius in the manuscript to indicate that he had experienced a vision of some kind on this occasion.

Reading this later, and thinking it was good to have written it out, a fresh devotion came upon me, not without water in my eyes, (V) and later, recalling these graces I had received, a fresh devotion.

In the evening, for an hour and a half or more, as I was going over the elections in the same way, and making the election for perfect poverty and experiencing devotion, I found myself with a certain elevation of soul and a deep peace, without the contradictory thought of possessing anything, and was relieved of the desire of proceeding any further with the election, as I had thought of doing a few days earlier.

The Annunciation of the Blessed Virgin.

8. Saturday [February 9].—The preceding night I felt greatly weakened because of a bad sleep, but the morning prayer was quiet, with sufficient devotion and a warm spiritual movement and a tendency to tears.

After getting up, the feeling of weakness left me twice. Later, in going to Mass, there was devotion in prayer, and also in getting ready to vest, together with a desire to weep. During Mass continual devotion and weakness, with different spiritual movements and a tendency to weep. The same when Mass was finished, and always with the determination to perfect poverty.

The day was quite peaceful, and, whereas, at its beginning I thought of keeping on with the election, all desire left me, as I thought the matter was clear, that is, to keep poverty perfectly.

At night, I went through the elections with much peace and devotion, thinking after all that we should have neither partial nor complete revenue. It was not a matter worthy of further thought. I looked upon it as finished. With much peace of mind, I remained firm in the thought of perfect poverty.

At this point, Ignatius had reached his tentative conclusion and was ready to offer it to God and seek divine confirmation of it. This he did on the following day, February 10, and more clearly and intensely on February 11. Signs of God's acceptance of the offered decision are given, signs so clear and so strong that Ignatius feels altogether secure in considering the whole discernment finished, with nothing left to do except to give thanks to God.

Mass of the day.

9. Sunday [February 10].—I went through the elections and made the offering of perfect poverty with great devotion and not without tears. Likewise earlier, in the customary prayer, before, during, and after Mass, with much devotion and many tears at the thought of perfect poverty. I was at peace when the offering was made, having understood very clearly when thinking about it, and later, certain feelings about my mediators accompanied by a certain vision (V).

At night, going over the elections between having complete or partial or no revenue, and making the oblation for perfect poverty, I felt a deep devotion, interior peace and quiet of soul, with a certain feeling of security that it was a good election.

Of the Holy Spirit.

10. Monday [February 11].—In the midst of my ordinary prayer, with no further thought of the election, offering or asking God our Lord that the oblation made be accepted by His Divine Majesty, I felt an abundance of devotion and tears, and later, making a colloquy with the Holy Spirit before saying His Mass, with the same devotion and tears, I thought I saw Him, or felt Him, in a dense brightness, or in the color of a flame of fire. Quite unusual, and with all this, I felt satisfied with the election I made (V).

Later, in order to examine and discuss the election I had made, I took out the reasons I had written down to examine them. I prayed to our Lady, and then to the Son and to the Father, to give me their Spirit to examine and distinguish, although I was speaking of something already done, and felt a deep devotion and certain lights with some clearness of view[.] I sat down, considering, as it were in general, whether I should have complete or partial revenue, or nothing at all, and I lost all desire to see any reasons. At this moment other lights came to me, namely, how the Son first sent the Apostles to preach in poverty, and afterwards, the Holy Spirit, giving His Spirit and the gift of tongues, confirmed them, and thus the Father and the Son sending the Holy Spirit, all Three Persons confirmed the mission.

At this point, greater devotion came upon me, and all desire to consider the matter further left me. With tears and sobbing, I made the offering of perfect poverty on my knees, the tears flowing down my face, sobbing as I made the offering, and later I could hardly get up for the sobs and tears of devotion and the grace I received. At length, however, I got up, and even then the devotion with the sobbing followed me, coming upon me because I had made the offering of perfect poverty, holding it as ratified and valid, etc.

Shortly after this, as I walked and recalled what has taken place, I felt a fresh interior movement to devotion and tears.

Not much later, as I was going out to say Mass, coming to the short prayer, I felt intense devotion and tears at realizing or beholding in a certain manner the Holy Spirit, and the election as something finished, but I was not able to realize or behold either of the other two Divine Persons.

Later in the chapel, before Mass and during it, there was much devotion and many tears. Later, great peace and security of soul, like a tired man taking a good rest, neither being able to nor caring to seek anything, considering the matter finished, except to give thanks, [pay some] devotion to the Father, and say the Mass of the Holy Trinity, as I had earlier thought of doing on the morrow, Tuesday.

Surprisingly, Ignatius did not, in fact, end his discernment on February 12. A disturbance and a temptation on that day initiated a long period of delay, a whole month. During that time, Ignatius experienced confusion, temptation to doubt the decision he had reached and to seek more confirmation. He finally came to see that seeking more confirmation was unreasonable, that he should have ended his discernment on February 12 instead of March 12. All that happened during the month after February 12 is interesting and valuable for studying discernment of spirits, but it would be a distraction from the clear preceding illustration of how to seek for God's will. For that reason I omit it.

FOUR

CASES WITH QUESTIONS FOR REFLECTION

● *Case 1* ●

1. I had been involved in my design business for ten years and had found it artistically satisfying and financially profitable. Since my children were all going about their own adult lives, I used this business to replace them. I became a compulsive worker. The business consumed most of my waking hours, and these hours became longer. The terrific stress of such work began to sap all pleasure from it; still, I worked on. God was in my life, but I paid scant attention to him. There was, of course, Sunday and a good moral life, but no acknowledged relationship with God other than that. My youngest daughter told me that I was a legalistic Catholic who was not a Christian. I protested, sometimes quite loudly, trying to defend my spiritual mediocrity. She prayed for me.

2. Many things started leading to Christ, too many to relate them all here. The most prominent was a sermon one Sunday at the cathedral. I began to be on fire. I actually began to pray daily (other than programmed prayer). It seemed stilted and foreign to me, but I remained faithful to it. I gave up television and began reading Merton.

3. In June I went on an eight-day retreat. That did it. I was in love. Now that my allegiance was sworn to Christ and his people, what, I asked myself, do I do with this bloodsucking business? I looked at it in every way I could think of; and, even though I had nothing in the wings that would replace it, I still felt and thought it was time to let it go. I went home and proceeded to start dissolving it. My husband couldn't quite understand any of this, but he did like the change in me and so made no effort to influence my decision.

4. I began my ministry of love by starting two Bible-prayer groups (billed as Praise and Thanks Groups) at a retirement center. I am now in my third year with them. I also began to facilitate two Bible-study groups at my parish. They did not have a program before this one. My next request from God was to have two groups on Saturday at the county jail, one for women and one (with a male partner) for the men inmates. My husband supported my missionary work; he was happy about it and I was overjoyed by it. All of this had been going on for quite a while. I was gradually being asked for more personal detachment, and I had been willing to respond.

5. Now, out of the clear blue came a phone call from Ed, a man I knew. He told me that the executives at his agency were no longer pleased with the style of the local designer and that they would like me to give a fresh and residential feeling to their executive offices. They had heard about my work and thought they would like this style. My response was, "It sounds wonderful, but I have retired, so I guess I can't do it." Ed proceeded, "They will give a generous retainer and let you have a free hand within an appropriate budget. We are redoing all the offices within the next three years and, of course, you are the choice for that also." By this time I was no longer in the moment. My dream button has been activated by the most exciting offer of my career as a designer. I found myself saying, "Yes, I will do it. Thank you for thinking of me."

6. I don't think I was off the phone more than ten minutes when physical symptoms began. I was breathing heavily. I almost felt sick to my stomach. My mind was screaming, What have I done? But, then, other thoughts came to me, encouraging me to follow through on what I had done: No one really cares whether I do these little ministry things or not; the church can get along very nicely without my efforts; the people will just gravitate to someone or something else; I won't even be missed. None of these thoughts were there before the phone call from Ed.

7. It seemed I had barely enough strength to telephone my friend in whom I had confided over the years. She had come home for a reason she couldn't explain until after my call. I told her what had happened and how horrified and depressed I felt. She calmly recited all the reasons I had given in the past for retiring.

8. My next call was to my daughter. When I told her the whole story, her comment about the "little despair" scenario was, "Mom, that is all lies. We both know the value of the things you are doing and why you are doing them." This stunned me. Suddenly all was clear. I felt peace again. Poor God, I am so shallow and faithless, and he still showers me with love and grace.

9. I hung up and was very certain of my next move: I would call Ed and gracefully decline. I told him I had been retired just long enough to be out of touch with my profession and promised to recommend another designer who would do a fine job for them.

➤ *Questions for Reflection*

[In these questions, the author of the case will be referred to as Ann.]

1. Paragraphs 1 and 2 lead up to the decision Ann makes in paragraph 3. In these paragraphs 1–3, do you think Ann is making a discernment of God's will? Why or why not? If so, by which of the three Ignatian modes?

2. In paragraphs 5–8, it is clear that Ann is facing a new situation which calls for her to make a crucial decision. Guided by the Ignatian rules for discernment of spirits, show how the events related in paragraphs 5–8 reveal the work of the evil spirit and the Holy Spirit influencing Ann toward her decision.

3. In paragraph 9, it is clear that Ann has come to a decision. Looking at paragraphs 6–8, do you see whether she came to that decision by the Ignatian second or third mode of seeking God's will?

Readings (in step 4 of "Method"): *Comm,* 30–33, 69–70, 152–55, 202–4, 238f.; *DGW,* 172–81

● *Case 2* ●

1. Marty had just recently graduated from college with a major in sociology, an intense interest in social issues, and a desire to work for the poor and oppressed. Several good opportunities were open to him. He decided to make a retreat to ready himself for this new phase of his life in closer union with Christ. During the retreat, especially at the end, he experienced intense and frequent spiritual consolations.

2. Immediately after his retreat Marty experienced an inclination to pass up the present opportunities for work in this country and go to work in the Third World, preferably far away in some exotic Oriental setting. He felt good about doing this. Since this inclination came so close to the time of his retreat with its spiritual consolations, he felt sure that the idea came from the Holy Spirit. It occurred to him that it would be wise to talk about this decision with his retreat director. On the other hand, he thought, this director had taught him that spiritual consolation is a sign of the Holy Spirit; besides, he thought, it's time for me to make my own decisions. After all, I am now an adult. So he decided that God was calling him and volunteered for service among the refugees in Thailand.

3. After a year of work in the Orient, Marty came home a physical and emotional wreck. Fortunately, prompt and excellent medical treatment and psychological therapy restored him physically and mentally.

4. In order to decide what to do now, he went to a retreat house to make the Spiritual Exercises. (He had heard about them from a

fellow worker in the Orient.) He had two main alternative projects in mind. The first was to return to work in Thailand and show that he could master the difficulties that had been too much for him the first time. The second was to get a graduate degree in sociology and work for the poor here in the United States. If he chose the second alternative, perhaps at a later time and in a different capacity he could go again to the Third World.

5. Early in this retreat, Marty received a surprising insight into what had happened in the discernment made immediately after his previous retreat. He saw clearly that the principal motivation behind his decision to volunteer for service abroad was not really the greater praise and service of God; rather, it was his own desire for adventure and excitement, for a chance to prove that he could do as much as others who were more robust. He was, however, still puzzled about the consolations which he had interpreted as signifying that the attraction to work in the Orient was from God.

6. The retreat director stressed that indifference to all but God's will was crucially important if one was to undertake a trustworthy discernment. When the director and Marty were confident that the latter had reached true indifference, he began the "election." When he set about drawing up the reasons on both sides for his two plans of action, he remembered not only what his physician had said but also what one of his teachers had told him, advice that he had disregarded during the previous discernment. His teacher had pointed out to Marty that he had extraordinary intellectual gifts and had done brilliantly as an undergraduate, that he would almost certainly work more effectively for the underprivileged as a professional sociologist than he would in any hands-on work with them, work for which he probably had neither the physical nor the emotional stamina.

7. Keeping in mind now what his physician and his former teacher had pointed out to him, Marty drew up and weighed the reasons for and against each of his alternative ways of serving God and his people. The case for going to graduate school and working in the United States seemed far stronger than the reasons for going back to the Orient. He also experienced notable spiritual consolations and, as an integral part of them, attraction to what reason indicated as more for the glory of God.

➤ *Questions for Reflection*

1. Applying Ignatian teaching on discernment of spirits and of God's will, how do you evaluate Marty's thinking in paragraph 2? What more than is said here would you need to know in order to evaluate his decision satisfactorily?

2. Did the turn of events related in paragraph 3 give clear evidence that Marty had made a defective discernment of God's will? Explain why it did or did not.

3. Does what Marty later uncovered (paragraph 6) about the motivation for his decision immediately after his earlier retreat show that the earlier discernment was defective? Explain why or why not.

4. Besides guarding against defective motivation in the first discernment, what other improvements do you see in Marty's second discernment in paragraphs 6 and 7?

Readings (in step 4 of "Method"): *Comm.*, 56–70, 222–35; *DGW*, 142–46, 216–29

● *Case 3* ●

1. Rebecca is in her senior year in college. She loves Christ very much and has been deeply affected by what she has read about the Church's option for the poor and about women such as Dorothy Day, the four women killed in Nicaragua while trying to help the poor, and other women who have dedicated their lives to working with and for the underprivileged and oppressed, even in the face of persecution and possible death. She feels a strong drawing to be with and to dedicate her considerable talents and energy to serving Christ in the poor. The drawing usually comes to her when her faith in Christ's love for her is vivid and her love for Christ is intense. She has uncovered a number of possibilities for serving Christ in the poor either in the single or the married state (if she can find a like-minded husband), or else as a consecrated celibate in a religious community. Right now, her question is whether to undertake one or another of these possibilities or to marry Robert.

2. For she is also very much in love with Robert, a handsome, charming, and thoughtful young man, who has asked her to marry him, preferably without delay. Robert is a very gifted young executive just entering upon a promising career in business. He ambitions going to the top in his field and having the power, wealth, and social status that go with such success. Although ambitious, he is not an irreligious or unethical man; he hopes to do some good for the world when he has gained wealth and power. But he has little understanding of or sympathy with Rebecca's ideals and inclinations; to him they seem unrealistic. He and Rebecca have talked about it; but Rebecca can see no way to reconcile

her altogether incompatible desires to marry Robert and to dedicate her life to serving Christ in the poor.

3. Frequently, when Rebecca is with Robert or when she is dreaming romantic dreams of their honeymoon and of raising children in a peaceful and tender home life, she experiences great delight and a strong desire for marriage with Robert. At such times the thought of breaking off her relationship with him makes her feel quite sad.

4. On the other hand, she frequently thinks about living with and working for the poor and oppressed; and at these times she feels Christ very close to her, feels unusually peaceful in the Lord. With these feelings she experiences an intense drawing to live with and for the poor and considers that it is to this kind of life that Christ is calling her. At these times, the thought of living in affluence with Robert and continually associating with a circle of people whose lives are centered on the values of wealth and social status makes her feel empty, depressed, separated from the poor and humiliated Christ.

5. These conflicting emotional experiences leave Rebecca quite confused, pulled in opposing directions, and unable to give herself fully to following either of them. If she only knew for sure which way God wanted her to go, she would surely go that way, she feels certain. But how can she know what God prefers for her?

6. Betty, a close friend in whom she confides, has heard a lecture on discerning God's will according to the teaching of St. Ignatius of Loyola. Ignatius, the lecturer said, taught us ways of seeking and finding God's will for our lives. According to the lecturer, feelings of consolation (joy and peace) with a drawing to one of the alternatives for choice are a sign that this drawing is from the Holy Spirit. On the contrary, feeling of desolation (sadness, emptiness, gloom, and so forth) with a drawing to one of the alternatives for choice are a sign that the drawing is not from the Holy Spirit but rather from an evil spirit. Applying this to Rebecca's experience, Betty says, it looks as if the delightful drawing to married life with Robert is from the Holy Spirit, whereas feelings of depression when thinking of breaking off from Robert brands that course of action as prompted by the evil spirit.

7. But, says Rebecca, what about my other experiences, when I feel great peace and joy along with a drawing to be with Christ in his poor and feel appalled at the prospect of a life of affluence and association with those whose main values are wealth, social status, and power? Why do I, at that prospect, feel far from Christ? Betty admits puzzlement and suggests that they look up the lecturer she had heard and see if they can find light from that source.

➤ *Questions for Reflection*

1. Is Rebecca's situation for choice one which Ignatius would see as suitable for applying his teaching on discernment of God's will? Explain.

2. In paragraph 6 of the case, what do you think of Betty's use of Ignatius's second-time mode of seeking to find God's will?

3. Do you find in paragraphs 1, 3, and 4 of the case any evidence to support either of Rebecca's alternatives for choice as God's will for her? If so, which one? Explain. If not, why not?

4. If you were the one from whom Rebecca and Betty sought help, what explanation and counsel would you offer?

Reading (in step 4 of "Method"): *DWG*, 130–60, 172–81, 251–54

● *Case 4* ●

[In his autobiography, as it is called, Ignatius tells of his early desire to go to Jerusalem and live as a pilgrim, praying at the holy places and being of spiritual help to others (¶¶8f., 35). When he finally got there, the Franciscan provincial, who held papal authority over pilgrims, told him (for very good reasons) to go home (¶¶36–47). The following is a very brief account of a crucial decision Ignatius made when he got back to Venice, and of subsequent events. These paragraphs are taken from his autobiography, as translated by William J. Young, S.J., *St. Ignatius's Own Story* (Chicago: Loyola University Press, 1956), ¶¶50, 54–56.]

1. After the pilgrim [Ignatius] understood that it was not God's will that he remain in Jerusalem, he kept thinking on what he ought to be doing, and finally felt more inclined to study so as to be able to help souls. . . .

2. . . . Returning to Barcelona he began his studies with great diligence. But there was one thing that stood very much in his way, and that is that when he began to learn by heart, as had to be done in the beginning of grammar, he received new lights on spiritual things and new delights. So strong were these delights that he could memorize nothing, nor could he get rid of them however much he tried.

3. Thinking this over at various times, he said to himself, Even when I go to prayer or attend Mass these lights do not come to me so vividly.

➤ *Questions for Reflection*

1. In paragraph 1, although he says only that he was "more inclined to study," it is clear that the inclination became a decision; for he immediately adds that he then made up his mind to go to Barcelona—to study, as is clear in the next paragraph. Is there any indication that his decision was the conclusion of a discernment of God's will? If there is, show it and show which of the three modes of discernment is indicated.

2. Do you find anything in the Ignatian rules for discernment of spirits which would suggest that the surprising spiritual consolation with illuminations described in paragraph 2 is prompted by the Holy Spirit? Do you find other rules that would more strongly point to the evil spirit as the prompting source?

3. Suppose that during and integral with the consolations and illuminations referred to in paragraph 2, Ignatius had experienced a drawing to give up studies and return to his former way of life, so like that of St. Francis. How then would you evaluate these experiences of consolation as evidence of God's will for Ignatius to change his previous decision to study?

Readings (in step 4 of "Method"): *Comm.*, 56–63; *DGW*, 216–29

● *Case 5* ●

[This case and the following one (case 6) are taken verbatim from John M. Perkins's account of his early life as given in his book *With Justice for All* (Ventura, Cal.: Regal Books, 1982), 19–21, 44–46. The paragraph numbers are added. For those who have not read the book, here is some brief background. Perkins passed his childhood in a broken family amidst oppressive poverty and inhuman violence, unsupported by any genuine Christian education in church or out of it. In his teens, Perkins fled Mississippi for California. There, after serving in the Korean war, he made good money, married, bought a large house for his family, and felt that at last his future was assured. At the age of twenty-seven, he was led to a serious interest in the Bible, and soon was sharing with others his new-found joy and strength derived from Christian faith. At this point a turn of events forced Perkins to face several very difficult decisions about his life. Here is his account as he wrote it.]

1. I began going with some Christian businessmen to share my testimony with the young prisoners in the prison camps along the

San Dimas Mountains. One morning, as I told about how I dropped out of school between the third and fifth grade and how God had come into my life and transformed it, two young men broke down and cried. After the session, I talked with them. They told me that their lives were much like mine and that they too wanted to know Christ.

2. As those boys shared their life stories with me, I began to think about my own values and goals. Many of these young men had backgrounds just like mine. Some came from the Deep South or were the children of families who came from there. They came to California just as I did, but for some reason they hadn't "made it."

3. Many of the problems in the ghetto, I was seeing, were really the unsolved problems of the South. This incident triggered a growing conviction that God wanted me to go back to Mississippi, to identify with black people there, to help them break out of the cycle of despair—not by encouraging them to leave but by showing them new life right where they were.

4. An inner battle raged for the next two years. On the one hand I had a growing hunger to go back to Mississippi and share this new-found love of God with my people. On the other hand I was afraid. We were just beginning to make it. After the Korean war I started with another company as janitor and worked up to a leadership position. I was motivated. I loved my job. What I really loved, I think, was the result of working—the money. I saved money and bought stock in the company. My stock divided twice while I worked there. I bought a big twelve-room house to raise my growing family. I was all set.

5. The lines of battle were drawn. Which would it be—the values of the world or sharing God's work in Mississippi?

6. I already had definite goals and was working hard to reach them. I didn't want to give those up. So I worked all the harder on my job, trying to drown out this call. But it wouldn't go away.

7. Another reason I didn't want to go was that I realized I was inadequate. One night I had this incredible dream. I dreamed I was preaching to a whole crowd of people in front of my house. That was really something—me preaching to all those people! Here I was a third-grade dropout. *No way* would I ever be preaching to all those people! And so I kept rejecting the call.

8. I remember when my growing conviction became a command. I was giving my testimony to a church in Arcadia, California. My text came from Rom. 10:1, 2: "Brethren, my heart's desire in

prayer to God for Israel is that they might be saved. For I bear them record that they have a zeal for God, but not according to knowledge."

9. God took the power of Paul's love for his people and shot it through me saying, "John, my desire for you is that you go back to Mississippi, because I bear your people witness that they have a zeal for God, but it is not enlightened."

10. I was reminded of the emotionalism of many of the congregations I had seen and heard. I thought of how little my people really knew about the Bible. It was true. My people had a zeal for God but not according to knowledge.

11. God was calling me. I could never be at home in California after that.

12. On June 9, 1960, we arrived back in Mississippi—the same Mississippi I had once left "for good." Vera Mae and I, along with our five children, went to live with her grandmother down near New Hebron.

➤ *Questions for Reflection*

1. In paragraphs 3–5 of the case, Perkins tells us how the alternatives for a crucial choice in his life took shape. What does he see as the alternatives?

2. Do you think these alternatives as Perkins expresses them in these paragraphs (3–6) are such as Ignatius requires for the kind of discernment of God's will with which he is concerned?

3. On the basis of paragraphs 1–3 and 7–8 in the case, can you suggest a way of seeing that the issue of choice facing Perkins—what he himself might also at times have regarded as his alternatives—would call for an Ignatian discernment?

4. Putting the question for choice in the way that calls for an Ignatian discernment, what kind of evidence do you think Perkins saw regarding his decision, first-time, second-time, or third-time evidence? Point out what you find in his account to substantiate your opinion.

5. Can you find in Perkins's account signs that when he terminated his discernment, it was truly in accord with Ignatius's way of thinking about such termination? That is, was it the right time to do so?

Reading (in step 4 of "Method"): *DWG*, 28–30, 108–11, 130–41, 158–60, 172–80

• Case 6 •

[After Perkins with his family arrived back in Mississippi and settled into his work for God, further situations arose for discerning God's will about choices to be made. One of these concerned Perkins's becoming a pastor, something he did not at all have in mind when he came. Thé most dramatic one, however, as well as the most painful and difficult, concerned what appeared to him as a choice between saving the life of his youngest son or staying with the good work he had begun to do in Mississippi. Here is his own account.]

1.   God's call to pastor a church was only one of several calls God has made in my life. I could never have survived our years in Mendenhall[, Mississippi,] without being sure God had called us to be there. There were times I wanted to leave. I wanted to bail out.

2.   One of the first such times came just six months after we moved back to Mississippi. We were still living in New Hebron with Vera's [his wife's] grandmother. Grandma's house, to say the least, was not the healthiest environment imaginable. We were crowded, we had no running water or nearby stream. Philip, our third child, started running a fever and limping. A local doctor prescribed medicine to relieve him, but Philip didn't get better; he only got worse. We wanted to take him to a specialist, but we didn't have the money. We didn't know what to do.

3.   Vera Mae began to get uneasy and started talking about going back to California. There I could have a well-paying job and we could afford medical care and a decent house and just possibly save Philip's life.

4.   Each morning during those days, I got up and went out to our church where I would pray in a back room. I usually read Scripture before I prayed, but on one morning I felt that God was pressing me to make a decision. On the one hand I felt that God had called us here. On the other hand my son was sick, getting worse and worse. In fact I had already picked out a grave site for him.

5.   The pressure on me was tremendous. As I knelt there before the Lord, the [question for] choice seemed clear-cut—stay where God had called me and bury my son or go back to California and save his life.

6.   As I picked up my Bible to read, it fell open to that passage where Peter said, "Behold we have left everything and followed you." And Jesus said, "Truly I say to you, there is no one who has left house or brothers or sisters or mother or father or children or farms for my sake and for the Gospel's sake, but that he shall receive a hundred times as much now in the present age . . . and in the world to come, eternal life" (Mark 10:28–38).

7. My feelings were probably much the same as Abraham's had been when God asked him to give up Isaac. God's will or my son—that was my choice, and right there we settled it—I would stay. I got up, convinced God would take Philip, but with a sense of peace, of release. I was going to do God's will. I went home and told Vera Mae, "I've given Philip up to the Lord."

8. [As a matter of fact God did not take Philip but saved his life. He became a healthy young man and a football star at Jackson State University.]

➤ *Questions for Reflection*

1. Based on paragraphs 5 and 7, what do you think were the alternatives for choice as Perkins saw the situation?

2. If Perkins's understanding of the alternatives for choice was as indicated in paragraph 7, did he have an issue for Ignatian discernment of God's will?

3. Given Perkins's history up to the time of this decision and given the objective situation that called for the decision, do you think his way of putting the alternatives for choice in paragraph 7 was the correct one?

4. Suppose the case were put this way. Each of the alternatives for choice is in itself good; Perkins does not yet know what, in this stressful situation, God wills for him to choose, but he must discern what God wills. Then, based on his account in this case, what evidence could you point out for thinking that God willed for Perkins to stay in Mississippi and carry on his mission for his people and what evidence for thinking that God wills for Perkins to return to California?

Reading (in step 4 of "Method"): *DGW*, pp. 28–30, 108–11, 130–41, 172–80

● *Case 7* ●

1. Rosalyn has been spiritual director to Gretchen for over a year and knows her as a woman growing in her Christian faith life and desiring to serve God in his people. Gretchen has been coordinator of religious education in a parish for several years now. In this work she has been very successful and is greatly valued by the pastor and the parish staff. However, she has recently been asked to take a position in pastoral ministry to the elderly. She feels an attraction to that ministry and possesses all the requisite gifts, so she wonders whether it is time

for her to move on to this new work. She comes to Rosalyn asking for her counsel on the matter.

2. Rosalyn suggests undertaking the Ignatian way of seeking God's will. She explains to Gretchen the essential dispositions for doing so and then the second mode of Ignatian discernment, by experiences of attraction or aversion during spiritual consolation or desolation. Gretchen spends some days in prayer to purify her intention, and when she seems to be truly indifferent to all but God's will, she begins observing and recording the relevant movements she experiences in prayer and at other times.

3. When she meets with Rosalyn, she reports the following experiences:

a. A number of times she has felt a drawing to continue as coordinator of religious education. The drawings came when she was feeling happy. Rosalyn asks her to describe the experiences. On one occasion, Gretchen says, she was happy because she received high praise for her work as coordinator. On another occasion, while at Mass with the youngsters, she had a sense of God's loving presence. At that time she experienced a deep peace because of her belief in God's love for her and them; with the peace came a strong desire that the children would all come to understand God's love for them.

b. Once she felt a strong aversion to the work of religious-education coordinator and with it a feeling of depression at the thought of continuing in it. Rosalyn asked why she felt that way and whether the depression in any way tended to diminish her Christian faith or hope or love. The reason for feeling as she did at that time, she said, was that she was tired and tense and had a headache after a particularly confused and unpleasant meeting with the staff. "After I had relaxed and rested," she added, "everything was all right again, I felt no aversion to going on with my work as coordinator."

c. Once, when visiting some old people, Gretchen related, she felt sad because they seemed so lonely; then she felt glad because she seemed to cheer them up. All this made her want to be with such people and make life better for them. Rosalyn asked, "Did you want to do so even if you had to leave work in religious education?" Gretchen replied, "Whether I should take the new position offered me and leave my present work as coordinator of religious education was not part of the experience."

➤ *Questions for Reflection*

1. In paragraph 2 Rosalyn explained to Gretchen the essential dispositions for any sound Ignatian discernment of God's will. State briefly (without developing) what these essentials are.

2. Consider the experiences Gretchen relates in paragraph 3a. Do you find in these any evidence that it might be God's will for her to choose continuing in her work as coordinator of religious education? Why or why not?

3. What about the experience related in paragraph 3b? Is this evidence against thinking God wills for her to continue as coordinator of religious education?

4. What about the experience in paragraph 3c? Is that evidence one way or another regarding God's will?

5. What next steps do you think Rosalyn should propose to Gretchen?

Reading (in step 4 of "Method"): *DGW,* 70–101, 130–60, 244–54

● *Case 8* ●

1. Rosalyn explained to Gretchen how to discern God's will by the third Ignatian mode and counseled her to undertake it and see whether she can find clearer evidence of what God wills. However, she recommended also that Gretchen continue to pray for and seek second-time evidence, while keeping the two modes of discernment and the two kinds of evidence clearly distinct. Gretchen did her best to follow Rosalyn's directions. After some days she presented the following reasons in support of each alternative, intending to review them with Rosalyn and examine whether they were valid third-time evidence.

2. The reasons for continuing as religious-education coordinator were the following:

   a. She has been very successful in this work. The pastor and the religious-education staff all want her to continue as coordinator.

   b. To form children for life seems to be a service of greater importance than the pastoral care of the elderly, who are for the most part securely settled in their religious life.

3. Gretchen's reasons for resigning as parish coordinator of religious education and accepting the position as pastoral minister with the elderly were the following:

a. She has a special gift for dealing with the elderly: a sensitivity to the particular beauty of the aged, a perceptiveness of their needs, compassion for their suffering, patience with their bad moods.

b. Pastoral work that is directly with people and involves personal relationships she finds more satisfying than her largely desk work as an organizer and director of the religious-education program.

c. She finds the old people so appreciative of what is done for them, so grateful for the attention shown them. This makes work with them more rewarding emotionally than her present work as coordinator, and she needs this.

➤ *Questions for Reflection*

1. What fundamentals of third-time discernment of God's will should Gretchen already know or have explained to her before beginning such a discernment process?

2. Do you see any important questions that Rosalyn needs to ask of Gretchen regarding her reasons (given in paragraphs 2 and 3) if these are to be considered valid evidence?

3. When the validity of Gretchen's reasons has been tested, what next steps should Rosalyn point out to Gretchen?

4. Suppose that after Gretchen has by second-time evidence come to a tentative conclusion and then by third-time evidence come to a conflicting conclusion, what should she do?

5. After settling what to do about the opposing tentative conclusions and then doing it, is there any further step for Gretchen to take?

Readings (in step 4 of "Method"): DGW, 70–98, 163f., 173–80

● *Case 9* ●

[This narrative is from Javier Osuna, S.J., *Friends in the Lord,* trans. Nicholas King, S.J. (The Way Series 3, 1974), pp. 136–38.]

1. After the middle of Lent, probably on the second of April, the six of them [Ignatius and his companions] came together to choose their superior in conformity with the Bull *Regimini militantis Ecclesiæ.* First of all they decided to prepare themselves by setting aside three days for each of them to commend the matter to God. They kept silence among themselves, avoiding discussion of the point with each other, so as not to influence one another. It was the method they had used in the 1539 deliberations. The document does not mention any exchange of

informationes, as was later prescribed for the election of the general. And that was reasonable, since they all knew each other so well.

2. At the end of the three days they met again, each one bringing his vote written in his own hand and sealed "so that each one would speak and declare his will with greater freedom." And "they were of the opinion" that they would put the bits of paper with the others which the companions had sent from Portugal and Germany. Then they put them in a locked box for three more days "for better confirmation of the matter." Presumably they could change their minds during this period.

3. On 8 April they had a further meeting to read the votes: "As they opened all the papers, one after another, all the votes fell to Inigo, *nemine discrepante,* except that Master Bobadilla (who was in Bisignano, and at the time of his departure for Rome was ordered by the Pope to stay longer in that city) gave his voice to no one."

Ignatius expounded his reasons quite candidly: He felt within himself "a greater desire and a greater will to be governed than to govern," he had not enough strength to rule himself, far less to rule others, and because of his many defects and past wretchedness he could not decide to take it on until he knew the Lord's will with greater clarity. So he begged them to consider the matter further for three or four days. "Although the companions were reluctant, this was decided upon."

4. On 13 April the election was repeated with the identical result. Ignatius, who in his profound humility really believed himself to be inadequate for the office, once again resisted the group's decision. And he decided to place the whole thing in the hands of his Franciscan confessor, Fr. Theodosio; he would make a confession of his whole life to him, and after declaring to him "all his bodily weakness and wretchedness," he would accept whatever answer he gave him. It was a real manifestation of conscience: the confessor, knowing everything, would have the last word in Christ's name. And from his verdict, "not a jot would be removed, even if the Pope ordered him to the contrary, as long as he was not assured of committing sin." From Ribadeneira we know the companions' reaction: "At this point they all started up in opposition, saying that God's will had been made sufficiently clear and they begged the blessed father not to put them off any more with his acts of humility, nor to postpone the business, since it seemed that he wanted to stand in the way of God."

5. Ignatius spent the Sacred Triduum at San Pietro in Montorio "making his confession to Fr. Theodosio and without coming near his companions. On 17 April, Easter Sunday, his confessor gave his answer: In his view Ignatius was resisting the Holy Spirit. He was still not

satisfied and asked his confessor to commend the matter further and to send his opinion to the Society in writing. On 19 April, the written reply arrived and was read in the presence of all of them, and Ignatius finally capitulated.

➤ *Questions for Reflection*

1. Ignatius's companions told him that "it seemed that he wanted to stand in the way of God." Fr. Theodosio told him that "in his [Theodosio's] view Ignatius was resisting the Holy Spirit." Would you agree or disagree with these judgments? Why?

2. Relying on what is said in this narrative, which of the three Ignatian modes of election (of discerning God's will) did Ignatius and Theodosio employ?

Reading (in step 4 of "Method"): *DGW*, 45–69

• *Case 10* •

1. Howard White, a Jesuit provincial, tells Jack Black, a member of the province, that he is being considered as the next local superior of a high-school community. He asks Jack to make a discernment about it and to report his conclusion and his evidence for that conclusion.

2. Jack seeks out his friend, Tim McDunn, to guide him through his discernment. (Tim has a reputation as an outstanding spiritual director and expert in Ignatian discernment.) Under Tim's guidance, Jack makes a serious discernment, observing carefully and generously all Tim's directives. To the question whether God wants him to be the new superior, Jack arrives at a clear and strong negative. He communicates his conclusion and an account of the evidence for it to Howard White.

3. The latter carefully considers Jack's account of discernment, seeks advice from his consultors, studies all the information about Jack and the needs of the community gathered from various sources, and makes his own discernment. The conclusion which he reaches is that God wants him to appoint Jack Black as the new superior. Accordingly he does so.

4. In a very upset state of mind, Jack Black calls Howard White. After all, he says, he had, as he had been asked to do, sought God's will through his discernment. Tim McDunn had assured him that his discernment was very soundly made and that he could trust the conclusion.

Therefore, either McDunn is not as competent a director as his reputation leads one to think and he (Black) really made a worthless discernment, or else the provincial himself had not really discerned or had discerned badly. In either case he is now opposing God's will.

➤ *Question for Reflection*

1. Do you think Jack Black's line of thought in paragraph 4 is convincing? If so, what should the provincial do about it? If not, explain why not and how Jack should think about this event.

Readings (in step 4 of "Method"): *DGW*, 45–54, 59–69

● *Case 11* ●

1. At a later date, during a social gathering of local superiors, Jack Black finds himself deep in conversation with Tullio Amico, sharing his experience prior to his appointment to his present job and explaining what he had learned through that experience about the limits of discerning God's will and about the role of consultative discernment. Tullio brings up a case he came across that seems to be in marked contrast to what Jack was saying about the limits of discernment. A certain highly respected superior general of a religious order, Father Sansouci by name, told a local community to elect their own rector from among their members. He would, he told them, approve beforehand whoᵢnever they chose—provided, of course, that it did not violate his conscience to do so. As things turned out, his conscience was at peace about the community's choice, and the man chosen by the community became their rector.

2. Based on what he had learned from his own earlier experience of discerning and from talking with others who knew more about it than he did, Jack Black tells Tullio that, in his opinion, Father Sansouci's way of acting was a cop-out. The superior general alone, he says, has the right and the responsibility to appoint a rector. Therefore he alone could make a trustworthy discernment about the matter. He might ask the community for a consultative discernment, as Howard White had done; but he could not turn over his responsibility to the community.

➤ *Question for Reflection*

Do you agree with Jack Black or do you think something is still missing in his understanding of discerning God's will? If the latter, explain.

Reading (in step 4 of "Method"): *DGW,* 55–59

● *Case 12* ●

[The following case is concerned principally with the important step of seeking confirmation of a decision already reached by discernment but held only tentatively until it is given divine confirmation. The case is taken from Richard J. Hauser's biographical account in his book *Moving in the Spirit* (New York: Paulist Press, 1986), 75, 77f. It is given in Hauser's own words but with a fusion of two paragraphs that are separated by several pages in his book.]

1. My experience of deciding to join the Jesuits illustrates many facets of these observations. In January of my senior year during a retreat I looked for God's will for my life after high school. I decided that God was calling me to go to college, become a lawyer and raise a good Christian family. I recall experiencing some relief at having finally come to a decision. This decision, however, was not confirmed by the Lord; the Lord did not hold my mind, will, and feeling toward it. As I reflect on it now, I can see clearly that the necessary conditions for seeking God's will were not present: I wanted to know God's will only if it confirmed my initial inclination toward going to college and getting married. I noticed that during this time my will was constantly pulled away from this alternative and toward the alternative of applying to the Jesuits. In addition I felt no inner peace much less sensible consolation and enthusiasm when I thought about going to the university.

2. Beginning in January of my senior year [after my retreat], I began experiencing consolation during prayer in a way I had never experienced before in my life. Indeed this was the beginning of my awakening to the Holy Spirit. I recall going up to church, sitting in front of the Sacred Heart altar and being absolutely overwhelmed. This was the first time I had ever experienced this type of enjoyment from being with God. And this consolation was present whenever I reflected seriously on the possibility of entering the Jesuits. If I began to lose this desire, I would simply return to my parish church, sit in front of the Sacred Heart altar, and again that consolation would be given me. Throughout this period I knew instinctively that this was the right

decision for me because of this consolation. I had not the slightest knowledge of a technical process for finding God's will or reflecting on my inner experience nor did I have the help of a counselor. . . .

3. . . . In March of my senior year, I finally gave up the struggle. I decided to apply to the Jesuit novitiate. From this time to when I entered the novitiate in August, . . . I consistently felt peace and sensible consolation whenever I reflected upon entering the novitiate. I intuitively judged that this peace was an indication that I was doing what was most right for myself.

4. However, as I reflect back on that whole process, I am convinced that it was very important for me to make the wrong decision first. It was only because the decision I made in January was not confirmed with the feeling of peace and consolation that I changed it. Had I not made that decision in January, I would have lived with the two alternatives constantly present in my mind and not have made a formal decision for either one. Most likely I would have drifted into college.

> *Questions for Reflection*

1. During his senior retreat in high school, Richard reached a decision that it was God's will for him to go to college and get married, but this decision was not confirmed by the Lord. In this context, what kind of confirmation was he needing and looking for, intellectual or volitional? Explain.

2. If he had received neither confirmation nor disconfirmation, should Richard have taken the lack of any response from God as equivalent to a disconfirmation? Why or why not?

3. If, as in fact he did, God disconfirmed Richard's decision, would that fact necessarily have indicated that the whole discernment to that point had been a defective one? Explain.

4. Richard speaks of his earlier decision to go to college and to marry as a "wrong decision" (paragraph 4). If lack of confirmation or even an actual disconfirmation does not justify thinking that his discernment was defective, can Richard find any good reason to think that the wrong decision resulted from a defective discernment process?

5. Does indifference as an essential condition for trustworthy discernment require that the discerner be totally free from any natural, spontaneous inclination toward either of the alternatives for choice, for instance, as in this case, free from any spontaneous, natural inclination toward college and marriage?

6. Suppose that after receiving confirmation and finalizing his decision, Richard had been accepted into the Jesuit novitiate. Then

suppose he found after a year that he was not fitted for the Jesuit way of life and discerned that God now wanted him to leave and go to college. Would that turn of events be a disconfirmation of the decision Richard had made when he decided that God called him to be a Jesuit?

Reading (in step 4 of "Method): *DGW,* 62–69, 191–232

●   *Case 13*   ●

[This case and the following one are accounts of vocation decisions written during retreat by two youths in nineteenth-century France. They are quoted in and translated from an article by Jacques Roy, S.J., "L'Election d'après Saint Ignace," *RAM,* no. 151 (1962): 322–23.]

1.   After serious reflection before God during this retreat, here are the motives urging me to believe that God wills to see me in the Company of Jesus. At the very moment of my first Communion I experienced a lively sentiment of love and of gratitude toward our Lord and a sort of inspiration to give myself wholly to him one day as he was giving himself then wholly to me. At least that is the most deeply imprinted memory of that day which remains with me.

2.   I believe I can say that since that day, whenever I felt more fervent and more united to God, I was animated by a like disposition. Whenever, on the contrary, I felt discouraged, more tempted to sin, I experienced at the same time a kind of disgust for the religious state of life and would tell myself that one can be an upright man and a very good Christian in the world [that is, living outside of the religious state of life]. But as soon as my heart was more elevated to God, I experienced something like a need of consecrating myself to him.

3.   The feeling of aversion showed up especially in my second year, and I believe that it has been my worst year of college. Nevertheless, I have never entirely lost sight of that interior inclination to give myself to God, and it has appeared more and more intense at the end of last year and during this year. I believe then that, in spite of my unworthiness, the good God has deigned to think of me in a special way.

➤   *Questions for Reflection*

1.   The young man who wrote the preceding account reported what he saw as evidence that God willed to see him in the Company of Jesus [the Jesuits] (paragraph 1). The evidence he reports clearly

derives from what Ignatius calls a "second-time for election" and it does seem plentiful enough. But to what is the drawing that is given with the spiritual consolation in these experiences? Does the description of these second-time experiences indicate a call to the Company of Jesus or is there a possibility that the discerner is being deceived? Explain what that possibility is.

2. What question or questions would you need to ask in order to reach clarity about the meaning of the experiences that are reported as evidence for finding God's will?

3. Making the supposition that the drawing experienced with consolation was to the Company of Jesus, do the experiences of disgust with an aversion to "the religious state of life" which came during times of discouragement and temptation have any significant role as evidence in this discernment? If not, why not? If so, why so?

4. If you were guiding this young man through his search for God's will, what would you advise after he had given you the above account?

Readings (in step 4 of "Method"): *Comm.*, 222f., 249–56; *DGW*, 130–60, 251–54

• *Case 14* •

1. Since my arrival in this house [the retreat house, that is], where God has led me so as to speak to my heart, these are the diverse states of my soul. In desolation as in consolation, the desire of practicing Christian perfection, of embracing religious life, has never for an instant left me. The only difference has been that the desire has been more or less intense depending on the diverse states in which I found myself.

2. If at times some memory of my worldly life has come to mind, if at times I have dreamed of the joys I have been able to taste in the midst of my family, such thoughts have not at all troubled me, because I am not in the least held back by them.

3. How often, when in trouble, have I not promised God that I would consecrate myself entirely to his service and that nothing could hold me back! Ah! then I felt comforted and I did not fear to say to God, "Do with me as you please. Never let me offend you anymore and let me serve you."

4. I cannot doubt that God calls me to religious life because his holy will is too plainly manifest, and I cannot prevent myself from exclaiming, "The finger of God is here!"

➤ *Questions for Reflection*

[The discerner's name in this case was Victor. As it stands, his statement of how he found God's will should, as in the preceding case, also be received with caution and examined to exclude the danger that adding something to the inspiration from the Holy Spirit might lead to deception. Leaving all that aside, the questions for reflections on this case will be directed to recalling and applying other elements in Ignatian teaching on discernment of God's will.]

1. If you were directing Victor through the retreat and he brought the foregoing account to you at the time of the "election," what inquiries would you think necessary regarding his consolations and the desires accompanying them?

2. Do you find at least some hint of what Ignatius speaks of as a first time for seeking God's will? Explain.

3. Assuming that Victor did have a first-time experience, does he need to reflect on it critically or does it exclude the need for any reflection? Would the evidence for a second-time or a third-time discernment have any value to Victor for finding God's will, or does the first-time experience eliminate the usefulness of any other evidence regarding God's will?

Readings (in step 4 of "Method"): *Comm.,* 109–21, 232–35; *DGW,* 107–29, 142–46, 156–60

•   *Case 15*   •

[Tonya, an American lay volunteer with Maryknoll Missionaries wrote this account of her experience. It happened while she was already working in Bolivia and waiting to go to Guatemala. At that time new circumstance arose calling into question whether it was God's will for her to go to Guatemala as planned.]

1. The initial decision of the Maryknoll director was for me to fill a job opening in Guatemala. Between the time of my acceptance and the actual going, fighting had escalated in that country. Letters from co-workers and superiors in Guatemala clearly stated that the violence would put limitations on ministry; I could expect to live in tension and stress. But the decision was left to me. If I still chose to go, I would be welcomed.

2. I sought counsel from people who had been there recently. Their comments ranged from "Sure, your work will be restricted, but

your presence will be important to the people" to "One would have to be crazy to go to Guatemala at this time."

3. I continued praying and gathering information, grateful that I didn't have to make my decision just yet.

4. When the deadline approached, I was no clearer about God's will in the matter than I had been two months before. What did God want me to do? I spoke to one of the authorities in the local area. He was angry that the superiors who sent me to Bolivia were not making the decision. He felt that, given the situation, it was their responsibility. I considered that since they were not telling me not to go, it meant it was all right for me to go. In fairness to me, so I thought, they just wanted to make sure I knew what I would be getting into. So, it seemed, I was right back where I started: Do I go or don't I? It's my decision.

5. By this time, I was truly agonizing over this decision. Out of desperation I spoke to another person; from our discussion the following reflections finally led to a decision:

a. I desire to do God's will, not mine. God's will *is perfect.* He would not steer me in a wrong direction. Totally certain of God's love for me, I can entrust my life to him. This became my premise.

b. But what if it is God's will for me that I *die* (a real possibility) in Guatemala? My death would probably come about in the same way as my birth—without any prior knowledge or consent. God has the right to give and take as he pleases. I certainly would not do anything that would jeopardize my life; but, actually, my life could end back home as I cross the street in front of my house. I do not know when or how it will happen. Just being in Guatemala does not necessarily spell death any more than not being in Guatemala ensures that I will evade death. All I can do is take all possible steps to preserve my life, but there are no guarantees. If God wills that my life should end in Guatemala, then I must accept it, believing that in God's perfect will my time has come. God is in control; and all I need to do is cooperate. Arriving at this point, I felt the burden lifting.

c. But the decision was not yet settled. It may be all right for me, but what about my family? I could not do this to my parents. They never wanted me to go to Bolivia in the first place. They would be devastated if I died in Guatemala. I had already disappointed them too much by leaving them. This would be the last straw.

d. On the other hand, if I believe God is in control and loves me and his will is perfect, should he not be able to take care of my parents? The basic question became, How far *does* his love and providence reach? I concluded that my death would have to be a matter between God and my parents. God would be there in their hour of need. And so I relinquished my hold on this too.

6. Now there were no more obstacles. There was no reason not to go to Guatemala. I would go. I went to sleep that night happier and more at peace than I had been in months. I was confident I would be doing God's will. I had come to this decision over a long time of prayer and thought and trusted that God had led me.

7. The following morning I received an overseas call from my superiors telling me I could not go to Guatemala. Random shooting was taking place in the area where I would be working, and the Sisters did not want me to go. I felt devastated. At first, I did not believe what I was hearing. I thought there was a mistake.

8. There was no mistake. It took a while, but eventually I was able to approach God once again. At first, I was very angry that God could do this to me. I felt he had made a fool of me. I had been told clearly that the decision was mine. I had carefully gathered as much evidence as I could (not an easy thing to do when you are in the Andes Mountains in Bolivia). I prayed constantly for guidance and wisdom. God led me to make an offering that astounds me now when I look back on it; but no sooner does my discernment reach a conclusion and the offer is made than I am told God does not want it. Why was I led down this path? What is the value of discerning God's will?

9. God's response to my reaction came in prayer. "You did exactly what I wanted you to do. Why are you so upset? You wanted to do my will and you did. You trusted me so much that you were willing to give up your life; you trusted me that I would even take care of your parents. That in itself is the beauty of the gift, and that is what I accept. It pleases me that you were willing to trust to the limit. Now, will you trust me about your not going to Guatemala? Will you trust me in this little thing?" It became clear to me how in an instant the prospect of dying had become easier than not going to Guatemala. What a truly strange and foolish creature I am. Thank God I have so patient and understanding a God.

➤ *Questions for Reflection*

1. Did Tonya seem to you to fulfill the essential conditions for a trustworthy discernment of God's will? Why or why not?

2. Did she bring her discernment to a conclusion too soon or too late or at the right time, that is, when the signs for concluding were present? Explain.

3. The order from her superiors forbidding her to go to Guatemala came right after Tonya's conclusion that God wanted her to go to Guatemala. Clearly, the superior thought that it was not God's will for her to go to Guatemala. Does not this fact imply that Tonya's conclusion was wrong and that her discernment was defective? Explain why or why not.

Readings (in step 4 of "Method"): *DGW*, pp. 62–69, 70–101, 158f., 212–15, 216–29

●   *Case 16*   ●

[The following brief account of a crucial decision by Fr. Richard Albert appeared in "I Never Meant to Be a Missionary," in *Mission* (New York: Propagation of the Faith, 1985), 5f. It is altogether too lacking in detail to allow for a certain judgment about what went on in this experience of seeking God's will; but it can serve as a good starting point for intelligent guessing and for playing with the case by making different suppositions—a way of becoming more proficient in understanding and applying Ignatian teaching on discernment of God's will.]

1. You know, I never meant to be a missionary. All my education pointed me to a life in campus ministry. But just before I was ordained, my superior said to me, "I want you to go to Jamaica and open our mission there." I thought he was talking about Jamaica, New York, and I said, "But we don't have any campus there." When I found out he meant the West Indies, I said an outright no. "No! I have no desire to be a missionary. I haven't been trained for it; it is nothing I want. No, and that's it."

2. "Well," he said, "take three weeks to think about it and then call me."

3. I got on the subway, going back to St. Ephrem's, where I was staying while in Brooklyn. It was midafternoon and the subway was very quiet. Suddenly I just started to laugh and the tears came to my eyes; I said to myself, Lord, you know, when you do things you do them in a roundabout way. So when I got back to the rectory, I got right on the phone and said, "Okay, I'm going." I knew in my heart that that's what the Lord wanted.

➤ *Questions for Reflection*

1. If Fr. Albert discerned God's will by any of the three Ignatian modes, which of them would you, off the cuff, guess to be the most likely one? Why?

2. What questions would you like to put to Fr. Albert in order to find whether your guess was correct?

3. Whatever the mode that Fr. Albert employed to discern God's will and arrive at his conviction, if he had consulted you about it before calling his superior, what would (should) you have advised him to do?

Readings (in step 4 of "Method"): *Comm.,* 216–21, 244–46; *DGW,* 107–26, 130–52, 161–81, 201–15, 251–54

● *Case 17* ●

1. Jenny is a young woman of superior intelligence with an educational background in science. She has a logical mind and a highly developed ability to question and analyze. Her experience supports her self-concept of one who can succeed at almost anything she tries. She is a good listener, able to help others with their problems through her skills of listening and insight.

2. During her college years, Jenny had given up the practice of her faith. Later, in graduate school her questioning led her to find new meaning in it, and she experienced God as present and active in her life. She found joy in praying the Hours and in regularly attending Mass. She volunteered her services at the Catholic Worker. She felt a strong desire to work with the poor and an attraction to join a religious community who worked for them. All of this was incomprehensible to her family and friends, but she went ahead, applied for admission to a religious community, and was accepted.

3. Her first ten months in the religious community found her in an almost continual state of uncertainty and confusion. She was agreeably surprised that she was able to form relationships with the other new members more easily than had ever before been the case at school or work; but this did not compensate for the fact that she now found prayer difficult, sometimes almost impossible. She felt that God was no longer with her or interested in her. The formation program's emphasis on reflection and introspection bothered her. She felt she had made a serious mistake in believing she could live this way of life. It seemed so divorced from the "real world." Others had religious experiences that

she did not. The most painful, the most depressing part of this confusing time was a profound disturbance at her seeming loss of faith and a temptation to doubt that God cared about her or even existed.

4. Despite all the dryness, desolation, apparent doubt, and turmoil, she was faithful to daily prayer; and her relations with others were usually sensitive and thoughtful, with only occasional outbursts of intolerance and irritability. She was generous in offering her time, talents, and energy to others. She was open with her director about her struggles and received support and love from the others in her community. She drove herself hard and plunged into all activities, often doing much more than was required.

5. During the brief and infrequent times of spiritual calm or of spiritual consolation, she continued to experience a deep conviction that God had called her here and wanted her to remain. About once a month she came to the decision that she should leave; but each time, after talking this decision over with her director, she returned to her earlier decision to remain. She again felt that God did want her here, that the decision to leave was a wrong one. During periods of peace she felt deeply that she should stay.

➤ *Questions for Reflection*

1. In this case, nothing is said about how Jenny arrived at her decision to join a religious community. The issue regarding God's will is confined to whether, once in religious life, Jenny should persevere or leave. Putting that latter issue for discernment aside for the moment, how would Ignatius's rules for discernment of spirits enable her to interpret what is going on in her spiritual life during her first months in the religious community?

2. Now, attending to the question whether God's will is for Jenny to leave religious life or to persevere in it, is there, in the account given in paragraphs 3–5, evidence to support either or both alternatives and, if both, for which alternative is the evidence stronger?

Readings (in step 4 of "Method"): *Comm.*, 56–70, 127–38, 141–44, 148–56, 182–91; *DGW*, 130–51.

• *Case 18* •

1. Helen, a theologically well-educated lay woman, sixty-eight years old and still vigorous, has served in many apostolates throughout

her life. For the past three years, she has ministered to the people of her parish through the rite of Christian initiation for adults (R.C.I.A.). Her ministry has been successful and rewarding not only for herself personally but also for the church. The people of the neighborhood view Helen as an example of faithful commitment to God. She is known not only for her faithfulness but also for her loving attitude toward all. Her classes in theology are exceptional. One might say that her knowledge, wisdom, and love come together to move the hearts of all her students.

2. God seemed very near to her and she experienced a deep trust and confidence in him. It was easy for her to see that God was close to her not only in prayer but also in her work. She was very contented in the Lord.

3. As the months went by, others became more involved in the program. Initially, Helen was enthusiastic about their involvement. However, these feelings began to change when she felt that they were taking over from her; she felt threatened, resentful, and confused. She wondered if she should continue her work in the parish. At times she thought of discussing this with her pastor or spiritual director; but fearing they might suggest that she retire, she kept her thoughts and feelings to herself. As time went by, she felt that God was becoming very distant. Prayer became difficult. She wondered if she was about God's work at all.

4. One night she attended a workshop at a nearby convent. The speaker talked about the importance of involving as many as possible in the various ministries of the parishes. While listening to this speaker, Helen felt a turning toward God, a sense of peace and gladness similar to what she had felt when others first got involved with her work. She wondered why she had been so self-centered and threatened by their collaboration. Consoled by these reflections, she felt willing to let others have the limelight. She even felt that it would be a loving and humble act to retire and leave the work to others. She took this as a sign that God willed for her to retire and let others take over.

➤ *Questions for Reflection*

1. In terms of Ignatius's rules for discernment of spirits I, 1 and 2, how would you classify Helen?

2. Among rules I, 3–14, which ones apply to what is going on in paragraph 3?

3. In paragraph 4, what spirit or spirits do you discern prompting movements in Helen? Explain.

4. What do you think of Helen's decision to retire? And what counsel would you give her?

Readings (in step 4 of "Method"): *Comm.,* 47–70, 122–38, 148–74, 182–91, 222–35; *DWG,* 70–86

• *Case 19* •

[The author of this account says that it was a real case (only the name is changed) and that he himself was the priest who helped David during his spiritual crisis (see paragraph 2). This priest at that time knew nothing about the teachings of St. Ignatius on discernment. (He wrote the following account of David's experience later on, while he was studying discernment of spirits and of God's will.) This fact might be the explanation of why he relates nothing much about what went on in the meetings with David other than what David said about himself.]

1. David has been an active member of the parish for several years. He is single, twenty-eight years old, a painter. He has been giving serious thought to becoming a priest. He is well liked by all the parish staff and enjoys the company of the priests, whom he regards as good models of what he would like to be. For several years he has volunteered to teach a sixteen-week course called Christians in Search. He excels as a discussion leader, able to lead people in prayer and shared faith.

2. (January) He approached each of the priests regarding his inner feelings of anxiety and turmoil. He complained of being unsure about his decision to become a priest. The issue was not celibacy or obedience to the institutional church; for at present he feels fairly comfortable with these elements in his life. "It's just that I don't know what to do," he explained. "I try to get priesthood out of my mind, forget about it, but I can't. But then I can't find any peace thinking about it either."

3. Aware of this inner angst in David, I suggested a regular monthly session for spiritual direction. David eagerly agreed. At the first meeting, he was very concerned about his prayer. It was very difficult, he said, and he had no energy. God seemed to have abandoned him and prayer no longer had meaning for him. "I don't think I can go on like this much longer," he said. "I don't know what to do."

4. (February) David canceled the meeting. "Nothing happening," he gave as his reason.

5. (March) He still had no answers. The negative feelings, he said, persist. He had pretty much determined not to enter the seminary the coming fall. Prayer was still very hard and God seemed so far away. He still taught Christians in Search, but wondered about moving or undertaking a new career. Nothing felt right for him.

6. (April) A week or two after our last meeting, David was sitting in his prayer chair at the usual time. Suddenly he was overcome by an overwhelming sense of the presence of God that flooded his whole being. "It was as if the entire room, in fact, the entire world, had changed," he reported. "I was filled with an overwhelming sense of God's incredible love for me. I also had at the same time an awareness of all that I had done wrong. I saw that my manner of praying was too self-centered: I always told God what to do or what I wanted, rather than seeking his will. All my problems, spiritual and personal, seemed to disappear in the enlightenment that was given. Peace and joy flooded me." There were tears of gratitude and happiness.

7. These feelings of profound peace and joy, intimacy with God, and experiences of love continued for several weeks; but that first moment of peace and joy was very special. His whole life after that had changed radically, and God's wonderful love was always very present and real, especially during prayer. He couldn't wait to tell his friends and enjoyed sharing with them this beautiful experience of God's love.

8. On Easter Sunday (about three weeks after the first experience of joy), David had another very vivid experience that seemed to flow from the first experience (paragraph 6). "It suddenly dawned on me," he said, "that my decision about what to do with my life had in fact already been made. I am. That's all. This is who I am and who I have been. It has been God's will for me; he gave me the desire to enter a seminary, and I will." This experience again brought David great peace and joy, knowing God's providence and loving care for him.

➤ *Questions for Reflection*

1. Assuming that David is a maturing Christian, do you see in paragraphs 2–5 any evidence supporting or casting doubt on David's possible vocation to the priesthood?

2. Do you see something in a later paragraph which indicates David's lack of a disposition that Ignatius counts as essential for trustworthy discernment? And do you see in the whole account a lack of something else, a lack that contributes to David's wavering and confusion?

3. What Ignatian rules for discernment of spirits help to understand David's affective mood in paragraphs 3–5 and the effect of this mood on his spiritual life?

4. What rules would give good counsel to David during the experiences narrated in paragraphs 3–5?

5. What rule or rules would apply to the experience related in paragraph 6? And what great grace was given with that experience which is of essential importance for David's discernment of God's will?

6. What rules illuminate the experiences related in paragraph 7 and what rules offer good counsel on how David should let these experiences be for his spiritual growth rather than a hindrance to it?

7. Does the experience in paragraph 8 describe or at least suggest one of the Ignatian "times for" and "modes of" finding God's will?

8. What counsels do you think anyone who was knowledgeable about and who followed Ignatian teaching on discerning God's will would have given David when he sought help (paragraphs 2 and 3)?

Readings (in step 4 of "Method"): *Comm.,* 56–69, 122–38, 147–204, 216–22; *DGW,* 70–86, 102–81

●   *Case 20*   ●

[The discernment told of in this case was a crucial one for the life of St. Francis of Assisi and the future of the Franciscan order. In order to include all the essentials of the event, I have conflated passages from two sources: Raphael Brown, trans., "The Little Flowers of St. Francis" and the account of the same event from the "Major Life of St. Francis," both in Marion A. Habig, ed., *St. Francis of Assisi: Omnibus of Sources* (Chicago: Franciscan Herald Press, 1973), 720–22, 1334f. Paragraph 1, 4–9, in my conflated version are from the "Little Flowers of St. Francis," and paragraphs 2 and 3 are from the "Major Life."]

1. The humble servant of Christ, St. Francis, at the beginning of his conversion, when he had already gathered many companions and received them in the order, was placed in a great agony of doubt as to what he should do, whether to give himself only to continual prayer or to preach sometimes. He wanted very much to know which of these would most please our Lord Jesus Christ.

2. . . . When he returned from where he had been praying, he put it before the friars who were closest to him, to have it resolved. "What do you think of this, Brothers?" he said. "Which do you think is better?

That I should devote all my time to prayer, or that I should go about preaching. I am a poor and worthless religious. I have no education and I am inexperienced in speaking; I have received the gift of prayer rather than that of preaching. Besides, prayer earns merit and a multitude of special favors, while preaching seems to be only a way of sharing the gifts that have been received from heaven. Prayer helps to purify the desires of the heart and unites a person to the one, true, and supreme Good, while giving an increase of virtue. The labor of preaching allows dust to enter into the soul and involves a lot of distraction and relaxation of religious discipline. In prayer we talk to God and listen to him and live a life worthy of the angels, with the angels for our companions. When preaching, we have to descend to the level of human beings and live among them as one of them, thinking and seeing and hearing and speaking about human affairs. But, on the other hand, there is one argument that seems to count more than all the rest in God's eyes, and it is this: The only-begotten Son of God, who is Wisdom itself, came down from the Father's embrace to save souls. He wanted to teach the world by his own example and bring a message of salvation to the men whom he had redeemed at the price of his Precious Blood, washing them clean in it and upholding them by its taste. He kept nothing for himself, but generously surrendered all for our salvation. We are bound to act always according to the model which has been set before us in him as on some high mountain; and so it seems that it is more in accordance with God's will that I should renounce the peace of contemplation and go out to work."

3. He discussed this problem with the friars over a number of days, but he could not make up his mind which course of action he should choose as being more pleasing to Christ. The spirit of prophecy had enabled him to penetrate the deepest secrets, but he was unable to solve his own difficulty satisfactorily.

4. So he called Brother Masseo and said to him: "Dear Brother, go to Sister Clare and tell her on my behalf to pray devoutly to God with one of her purer and more spiritual companions, that he may deign to show me what is best: either that I preach sometimes or that I devote myself only to prayer. And then go also to Brother Silvester, who is staying on Mt. Subasio, and tell him the same thing."

5. Brother Masseo went and, as St. Francis had ordered him, gave the message first to St. Clare and then to Brother Silvester. When the latter received it, he immediately set himself to praying and while praying he quickly had God's answer. And he went out at once to Brother Masseo and said, "The Lord says you are to tell Brother Francis this: God has not called him to this state only on his own account, but

that he may reap a harvest of souls and that many may be saved through him."

6.   After this Brother Masseo went back to St. Clare to know what she had received from God. And she answered that both she and her companion had had the same answer from God as Brother Silvester.

7.   Brother Masseo therefore returned to St. Francis. And the saint received him with great charity: he washed his feet and prepared a meal for him. And after he had eaten, St. Francis called Brother Masseo into the woods. And there he knelt down before Brother Masseo; and bowing his head and crossing his arms, St. Francis asked him, "What does my Lord Jesus Christ order me to do?"

8.   Brother Masseo replied that Christ had answered both Brother Silvester and Sister Clare and her companion and revealed that "he wants you to go about the world preaching, because God did not call you for yourself alone but also for the salvation of others."

9.   And then the hand of the Lord came over St. Francis. As soon as he heard this answer and thereby knew the will of Christ, he got to his feet, all aflame with divine power, and said to Brother Masseo with great fervor, "So let's go—in the name of the Lord!"

➤   *Questions for Reflections*

1.   As far as we can tell from this story, before Francis sent Masseo to Clare and Silvester, which of the three modes mentioned by Ignatius for seeking to find God's will did Francis employ in his own effort to find the answer to his question? Why do you think so?

2.   We do not know what went on in the prayer of Clare and Silvester; but just considering both their responses to the question from Francis, is there any indication of the mode of discernment by which God led them to their conclusion? If so, what?

3.   Do you think the discernment by Clare and Silvester was consultative or delegated? What reason do you have for your answer?

4.   If their discernment was delegated, do you think Francis was justified in delegating the discernment and acting on the conclusion reached by Clare and Silvester? Explain why.

Reading (in step 4 of "Method"): *DGW*, 50–56, 108–13, 130–38, 161–68

• *Case 21* •

1. Sister Eileen is a university teacher in her forties, just reaching her best years in academic work. Her provincial superior asks her to undertake a consultative discernment about God's will regarding her appointment as novice director. The present director, says the provincial, has become too ill to continue in the position, and there is no one other than Eileen available who could immediately fill that position; all others would require at least two or three years of preparation. The number of novices and other factors would demand that Eileen leave the university for some years.

2. Eileen takes a month to pray, to read the relevant documents, and to consult with some friends who know her well and whose judgment she respects. Her friends all agree that she should accept the appointment. Their reasons are these: *(a)* there is hardly anyone else capable and available, *(b)* she has with evident competence been giving directed retreats and spiritual direction for six years and written well-received articles on prayer, *(c)* she understands the history and spirit of the community, and *(d)* she has herself been faithful in prayer and lived according to the spirit of the community.

3. After a month, Eileen meets with her provincial. She reports what her friends have advised and admits that they have a point.

4. On the other hand, her reading and reflection led her to think she is not fully prepared for the proposed assignment. She thinks she needs more study in psychology, counseling, and history of spirituality, along with some clinical-pastoral education and some training in giving spiritual direction. For these reasons alone she would be uncertain about undertaking the new work.

5. But what makes her quite certain that God is not calling her to it is the fact that she has not experienced in prayer any clear drawing toward it, no peace and joy in the thought of it. Rather, she feels troubled, even discouraged and a bit resentful sometimes, at the thought of leaving her work at the university, of losing the tenure that has just been granted to her, of having to leave unfinished a book she is writing. If God were calling her to be novice director, would she not experience a strong and clear attraction to that work, along with much peace and joy at the prospect?

6. Besides what she sees as evidence against her being the director of novices, Eileen also sees what she takes to be positive evidence for continuing in her present work: she feels strongly drawn to stay in university work and feels peace and joy at the thought of doing so. Is this not a sign of where God is calling her?

➤ *Questions for Reflection*

1. What reasons based on objective facts (third-time evidence in Ignatian terms) does Eileen have for judging that God wills her to give an affirmative response to her provincial's proposal? How would you critically evaluate these reasons?

2. What evidence of this same kind does she have for judging that God wills her to give a negative response?

3. If Eileen asked you for your opinion about which set of evidence you would consider weightier, how would you answer her?

4. However the opposing sets of reasons may be evaluated, Eileen states in paragraph 5 what is for her the decisive evidence. Do you also consider this evidence decisive? Why or why not?

5. Is there any indication in paragraph 5 that Eileen has not fulfilled one of the essential conditions for a sound and trustworthy discernment?

6. Does what is said in paragraph 6 serve as sound evidence for God's will?

7. What counsel should Eileen be given on how to meet the present situation, which calls for a decision without very much delay?

8. What counsel should be given for the long run, especially if Eileen is to become novice director or if she is, in any case, to develop as a spiritual director?

Readings (in step 4 of "Method"): *DGW,* 70–86, 98–106, 130–76

● *Case 22* ●

[During a conversation that I had with a man (let us call him Charles) who was an eminent director of the Spiritual Exercises and teacher of Ignatian spirituality, he told me what he had once experienced in his youth, shortly after he had applied to the Society of Jesus but before going to the Jesuit novitiate. Some time after our conversation, I wrote to him and asked him to put the story in writing for me. The first two paragraphs in the following account are taken from the letter that he wrote in response to my request.]

1. Now to your inquiry: the experience you asked about happened in church during my little sister's confirmation. The experience came as a flash from the tabernacle—very brief, almost like a photoflash [but not, as he had told me in our conversation, a sensible experience].

There were no words. The idea conveyed preceded any words. The meaning was immediately clear and needed no discernment, no development. There was no warmth, no notable spiritual consolation, just an assurance that I had made the right decision. For I had already applied for admission to the Society, although I cannot now remember whether or not I had received my answer. Thus it was not really a "call" so much as an approval of a choice already made. In fact, I wonder if I had even thought in terms of a "call." I had prayed a lot to make the right choice and had been motivated mostly by a desire to spend my life more usefully than as a clerk in an office, the kind of work I had been doing for five years since high school.

2. Subsequently I have never doubted the reality of the experience or its meaning, but I did forget it for long periods. In my first months in the novitiate, I underwent a severe temptation to leave, but as far as I can recall I had no recourse to the experience or even remembered it. During a few later and milder temptations as a scholastic, I again failed to use the experience, but I cannot be so sure of this.

[Since what my friend related to me sounded so much like a "first-time" experience, I wrote again to inquire whether in the experience he had related there was any drawing such as Ignatius mentions in his description of a first-time experience in the Spiritual Exercises, ¶175. In his next letter he responded as follows.]

3. About my experience: as far as I can remember, the volitional element was absent or at most was so weak as not to impress itself on me. I thought of it simply as an illumination, an assurance, a confirmation. I cannot recall anything like a *drawing*.

➤ *Question for Reflection*

Do you think Charles's experience, as he describes it, is or is not what Ignatius would name a "consolation without previous cause" or a "first time" for election—or what? How would you justify your opinion?

Readings (in step 4 of "Method"): *Comm.*, 216–21; *DGW*, 107–27, 192–94, 205–10

• *Case 23* •

1. Patrick has been a member of an actively apostolic community for about twenty years.

2. For the last two years he has experienced a recurrent, almost continual drawing to be more with God in prayerful solitude. Without neglecting his duties, he has spent all the time he can alone in prayer. Because in his present circumstances he cannot always yield to the attraction, it has sometimes been painful, but always with spiritual peace.

3. Frequently also during solitary prayer, more often (surprisingly) at other times, he unexpectedly experiences God's overwhelming presence and love and is moved to intense love in return. This happens, for example, when driving, when grocery shopping, when counseling or teaching. These spiritual experiences do not interfere with such activities; in fact, they help counseling and teaching. These experiences come without anything leading up to them. Even when they come during prayer, they do not seem to arise from what has been going on in his prayer. When he has these experiences, Patrick also feels drawn to give himself and his whole life totally to God, to "let go of everything" for him.

4. After these surprising experiences of divine presence, everything else seems dull and insignificant by comparison.

5. Patrick thinks that God is calling him to a more purely contemplative life and that he should be doing something about it, that he should be discerning where God wants him to go in order to live such a life, for example, to the Carmelites, the Trappists, or the Carthusians.

6. He has talked over the whole matter with his religious superior. The latter has listened with an open mind, concerned for Patrick's good. He suggested making arrangements within the community for Patrick to have more solitude and time for prayer. Patrick, however, thinks that doing this would make him singular and disturb others.

7. At this point Patrick consulted with someone who he thought had enough experience and learning in discernment to be helpful. This counselor inquired first about Patrick's relationship with his present religious community and about his work. He found that Patrick genuinely loves the congregation, that he has a very good relationship with the members of his local community, that he is cheerful and finds his active ministry a good one. Further, he has in a spirit of obedience and loyalty accepted every assignment given him, worked hard at it, and seemed to be effective in his work. He thinks he has been able to grow as a Christian and serve God and his neighbor in his present way of life.

8. Then the counselor asked Patrick to reflect very carefully before answering two more questions. First, regarding the rather continual drawing he has felt to a more contemplative life, was he being drawn explicitly toward a life without active ministry, in a purely contemplative community? Patrick thought silently for some moments and then replied, "No, the idea of a purely contemplative life in another commu-

nity is my interpretation of the attraction I experienced; I just assumed that the drawing to a fuller life in prayer meant a purely contemplative life."

9. A second question from the counselor concerned those times when Patrick had sudden, overwhelming, unexpected experiences of God's loving presence, during which he felt drawn by God "to leave everything for him" and give himself totally to God. Did that drawing, the counselor asked, explicitly involve leaving your present community in order to begin a new way of serving God free of active ministry? Again Patrick thought and again replied that the drawing did not explicitly include this course of action; the thought of doing so was rather something that came to him afterwards, in reflection on the experience. It seemed to him a clear conclusion implicit in leaving everything and giving himself to God.

➤ *Questions for Reflection*

Presupposing (with good reason) that Patrick is a spiritually maturing person, answer the following questions in terms of Ignatian teaching on discernment of spirits and of God's will.

1. What do you make of Patrick's experience described in paragraph 2 of the case? Is God the source of this attraction?

2. What do you make of Patrick's experiences described in paragraph 3 of the case? What Ignatian rules for discernment of spirits apply?

3. What value do you see in the information brought forth in paragraph 7 by the counselor's questioning?

4. Regarding Patrick's answer to the counselor's question in paragraph 8 of the case, what Ignatian teaching could the director profitably explain to Patrick and apply to his experience?

5. Regarding Patrick's answer to the question in paragraph 9 of the case, what Ignatian teaching could profitably be explained to Patrick and applied to his experience?

6. In view of the information derived from the counselor's questioning in paragraphs 7–9, what should be said of the interpretation that Patrick, in paragraph 5, put on the experiences described in paragraphs 2–4 of the case?

Reading (in step 4 of "Method": *DGW,* 42–152; *Comm.,* 213–56

● *Case 24* ●

1. Paul is a gifted and energetic man, active in business, in civic life, and in his parish. He is a devoted husband and father.

2. Paul has been asked to work on a project that will promote good race relations in the city. Since he already has as many commitments as he can comfortably handle, he does some serious praying and deliberating for a few days to decide whether to drop out of another work he is doing in order to take up this new one. He really doesn't like the idea of letting go of any projects he has already undertaken, but he wants to find God's will in the matter. Under different aspects he finds reasons supporting each of the alternatives, but in the final analysis the reasons for what he is already doing seem to him a little stronger.

3. However, during the days of prayer and deliberation, Paul perceived frequent, deep, intense and joyful indications of God's loving presence and care for him, along with a peaceful desire to serve God with all his might. Each time this experience came, he also felt a strong drawing to undertake the new work to which he has been invited.

4. What should he make of this situation? On the one hand, he cannot help feeling that the spiritual experiences inclining him toward the new work might have some significance, even though he doesn't know why. (As yet he knew nothing about discerning God's will by experiences of attraction and spiritual consolation.) On the other hand, his deliberation had indicated that what he is already doing is the better choice. In this hesitating state of mind, he seeks counsel.

➤ *Question for Reflection*

If Paul came to you for help, what would you do to help him reach a decision?

Readings (in step 4 of "Method"): *DGW,* 71–86, 130–47, 163f., 173, 270f.

● *Case 25* ●

[Let us assume that Paul finally decided to undertake the new work proposed to him, to which his spiritual experiences inclined him (see the preceding case).]

1. Sometime later Paul receives a request from the governor of the state to work with a group he is appointing for a project that will very likely be of great benefit to poor and underprivileged persons. This

time, Paul cannot drop any of his other important responsibilities, and accepting a new one seems quite unreasonable: he would not be able to give it the time and energy it deserves and he would put too great a strain on himself. Besides, he knows that there are others who could do the job at least as well as he could.

2. He is about to refuse the governor's request when during prayer he remembers all the extraordinary gifts from God in his life. He is moved to gratitude for God's love shown in the gifts and to immense joy in God's love for him. He is also moved to deep compassion for those who have so much less given to them and whose path in life is so arduous. He feels strongly inclined to say yes to the governor after all. So he hesitates.

3. During the next few days, he finds moments from time to time for more reflection and prayer. He has no more experiences of spiritual consolation such as the one that caused him to hesitate about saying no to the governor. What is more, the reasons against an affirmative response to the governor appear even stronger than they seemed to be at first. Besides the reasons he already thought of (paragraph 1), he thought of another very obvious and strong reason: if he took on this new work, he would not have sufficient time to spend with his wife and children, all of whom need his presence very much at this juncture in their lives.

4. On the other hand, however, remembering what he learned on the earlier occasion about the significance of spiritual consolation and drawing for revealing God's will, he thinks that after all God does want him to follow through on the inclination he had the other day when he was in great consolation.

5. Before calling the governor to say yes, he figured he had better be on the safe side and check out his decision before acting on it.

➤ *Question for Reflection*

If Paul again came to you and told you the whole story, what would you say to him this time?

Readings (in step 4 of "Method"): *Comm.,* 222–35; *DGW,* 70–86, 142–47

• *Case 26* •

[Assume that Paul finally said no to the governor (see case 25). What follows here is more a matter for discernment of spirits than of

God's will; but it is relevant to our study of discerning God's will because it deals with an experience that follows on such a discernment and has at the core of it the decision reached by that discernment. It calls into question the value of Paul's previous discernment of God's will.]

1. For a time after his decision to refuse the governor's request, all goes well, and Paul is glad he had decided as he did. Then one day he has another spiritual consolation very like the one he had when deliberating about the governor's request. Again, reflecting on the many good things in his life as manifestations of God's love for him, he experiences a joyful movement of love and gratitude, along with profound and tender compassion for the poor, the oppressed, the handicapped. Immediately after this experience, he remembers the former one and the impulse that came with it, the impulse to say yes to the governor. He begins to feel anxious. Did he after all, go against God's will in the decision he then made? If he did, can he do anything about it now? He wonders whether he is and all along has been acting selfishly, merely going through the motions of seeking God's will while really only doing his own will. Is anything he is doing really done for the greater glory of God? Does he really care about the poor and the suffering or does he just enjoy having noble feelings? He begins to be gloomy and irritable. If he is the selfish sort of man he now suspects he is, he asks himself, then how can God really love him? Maybe the sense of being greatly loved by God is merely an egoistic fantasy.

2. He wants to talk to someone about what is going on in him, but feels it would be an imposition on the other and a grave embarrassment to himself. Perhaps he had better stand on his own two feet and work through his confusion and anxiety by himself. However, his efforts only lead to worse confusion and emotional disturbance. In desperation, he finally comes to you and tells you what has been going on.

➤ *Question for Reflection*

What would you do to help Paul understand what he has been experiencing and to overcome his confusion, his anxiety and the temptation to doubt the validity of his previous discernments of God's will (cases 24 and 25)?

Readings (in step 4 of "Method"): *Comm.*, 56–70, 109–15, 127–38, 222–35, 150–74

• **Case 27** •

[The following description of a series of related spiritual experiences are from two letters written by the woman involved. Let us call her Pauline. The events described in paragraphs 1–5 took place when Pauline was still very young.]

1. I was in our living room scanning our Catholic weekly newspaper when I came across the prayer of St. Ignatius, the *Suscipe*. Interestingly, I was doing this only because there was nothing else to do at the time. When I got to the words of the prayer, "Give me your love . . . with that I am rich enough," an interior command seemed to take hold of me, one which I can only try to describe in this way. I heard no words, but I seemed to know what I was to do: Stand up, fold the newspaper, go to my room. This I did. When I got to my room, the interior command continued: Shut the door, kneel down. When I did this, my soul was invaded by an onrush of a power I could never describe. Something was poured into me that brought on a torrent of tears; and I just said, "Give me your love, give me your love," over and over again. When I "recovered" I just went back to my old way of living, which was dominated by the philosophy of following the way of least resistance and enjoying fun-filled weekends.

2. A little more than two years later, I had several similar graced experiences in which I received a call to the vowed life of poverty, celibacy, and obedience in a religious community. There was a series of three "touches." These experiences, which I call my "vocation graces," were spread over most of the year. They were separate from the *Suscipe* experience. (Although my discernment made much later in life regarding the hermitic call has brought them all together.) I should really call them three bolts out of the blue.

3. In the first one I was sitting on my bed putting up my hair, when suddenly a strong "power" took hold of me and I found myself calling out to my roommate, "Mary, I have a vocation." [As indicated in paragraph 2, vocation here means a call from God to the vowed life of poverty, celibacy, and obedience in a religious community.] This was accompanied by a torrent of tears. In total bewilderment I just kept repeating, "I have a vocation." It was quite the episode for Mary, I guess; for the next day she sheepishly asked me about "my vocation," and I had so completely gotten over the experience that I had to be reminded. When I did recollect it, I just brushed it away and said, "Oh, that—there is nothing to it," or words to that effect.

4. Shortly after this it happened again. (These two graces happened sometime between early spring and July of the same year.) As before, I was putting up my hair, getting ready for bed. I cried out

again to my friend saying the same thing, "I have a vocation." This time she didn't ask me about it again the next day, probably because I obviously looked as if I had again forgotten the whole thing. (Perhaps she was seriously doubting my mental stability.)

5. The following January (January 2, then the feast of the Holy Name of Jesus), I was alone in the kitchen of my parents' home, finishing up the supper dishes, when again the "sudden something" took hold of me. I wish I could describe it, but I cannot. I remember being so affected by it that I had to grab the sink with one hand and the stove with the other (it was on the other side of our narrow kitchen). Again tears. This time I knew the change had happened—that it was permanent and unmistakable. I could not doubt the "message" of the encounter even if I wanted to. I don't know how this knowledge was so certain; but as soon as I "recovered," I called my sister long distance to inform her, "I have a vocation." I never would have done that if I had thought that the effect of the experience would be gone in the morning. The conviction of God's call to me did not go away and has remained to this moment.

[In response to God's call, Pauline did apply to and was accepted into a contemplative religious community. After many years of contented life in this community, she experienced another call from God to live as a hermit. The discernment of this call extended over several years. She tells of this discernment in the following paragraphs.]

6. What I would like to add is that one of the greatest graces I have received was my almost being forced (out of desperation) to employ the Ignatian process of discernment (the "election") [regarding my call to the hermitic life]. In studying this process and placing myself before it as a pupil, I grew in my understanding of the intimate presence of a God who is like a father taking the hand of a child and teaching her to walk. This time, he wasn't going to give his grace "of a sudden," but he wanted me to use my intellect and reasoning powers. Nevertheless, it was really God in the beginning, in the middle, and at the end, gradually and gently leading me to understand his will. The Ignatian method is embarking on a covenant relationship with our Lord. I am grateful. [Nothing is said here by Pauline about the process. In a conversation with me, however, she made it very clear that her decision rested on both the second and third Ignatian modes of discernment, that is, on spiritual consolations with clear drawings to hermitic life and an objective reasoning about whether such a way of life would be *for her* a better way of serving God and God's people.]

7. This discernment of my hermitic call has come to a conclusion in these past several years and has shown me the continuity of every-

thing in my call from the beginning to the end. When I began the Ignatian process of discernment (paragraph 6), I received what I think was an understanding of my *Suscipe* grace. Until that moment I had always thought of it as only an encounter with God in which he granted me the prayer of petition, to ask for greater fullness of his love. I still think that, but with further understanding. My being "sent" to my room, I now realize, was a "protograce" of my hermit vocation. When this thought came to me, I remember how awestruck I was and how very simple the whole picture became. I was already alone in the house when the event happened, so I didn't have to go to my room for privacy. Of course, here I could be wrong, but I seemed to experience a great deal of peace about this conclusion. I know I did not conjure it up, because I never felt the need to scrutinize this *Suscipe* grace further. Although discernment regarding my hermitic life was fully distinct from the three vocation experiences I related above, I did see clearly that the "vocation graces" were a part of the whole call from God. A univocal constant in all this has been a call to the contemplative way of life. The earlier choice just never totally answered the call.

8. Recent developments have commenced to place me in another state of awe. I don't know if you remember my mentioning to you my seeking a place for my hermitage in connection with the apostolate of making known the doctrine of divine mercy. (You asked if following my call was concretely possible.) I don't want to burden you with the details; but not only is there a place to go, but it fits in exactly with what God has been forming in my soul—meaning to be a hermit of divine mercy. One of its main features is living in solitude imploring God's mercy upon the world.

➤ *Questions for Reflections*

1. Some questions regarding Pauline's *Suscipe* experience narrated in paragraph 1.

    a. Among the spiritual experiences to which Ignatius refers in his rules for discernment of spirits, to which one do you think Pauline's "Suscipe" experience most fully corresponds? Why do you think so?

    b. Was this experience evidence of God's will regarding Pauline's choice of a state of life?

    c. In light of what is said further on, does this *Suscipe* experience have anything to do with the author's vocation decision?

2. Some questions regarding the "three touches" mentioned in paragraphs 2–5.

 a. Which time for and mode of election in the Ignatian scheme does the third touch (paragraph 5) seem to fit? Explain your answer.

 b. What about the first and second touches described in paragraphs 3 and 4? Do they also fit in the same mode of discernment as the third touch? If not what do you make of them?

 c. Is anything said in the account of the three touches which justifies concluding that Pauline was called to be a cloistered contemplative?

 3. What about the development described in paragraph 8? Could it constitute a confirmation, in any sense of that word, of an already finalized conclusion of the discernment about the hermitical life? If so, in what sense could it have done so and in what sense could it not have done so?

Readings (in step 4 of "Method"): *Comm.,* 216–21; *DGW,* 108–13, 192–94, 221f.

FIVE

PROPOSED RESPONSES
TO THE QUESTIONS FOR REFLECTION

• *Responses to Questions for Case 1* •

1. It is clear from paragraphs 1 and 2 that two events brought Ann face to face with a hard and crucial question: her conversion from spiritual mediocrity and her awareness of the negative influence her designing business had been exerting on her relationship with God. The question for decision was, What do I do with this blood-sucking business? In the context, the question can reasonably be transposed to read, What does God want me to do about the business?

She gives no details about how she arrived at an answer to her question; but, given the context, what she says in paragraph 3 points to the third Ignatian mode of seeking God's will: "I looked at it in every way I could think of." In other words, she looked at all the ways in which the business could be a help or a hindrance to a life of deeper union with God and of greater service to his people, to being a true Christian. Weighing all these, freedom from the demands of the business that devoured her attention, time, and energy appeared to her to be clearly more for the glory of God than continuing to carry on the business.

2. There is no need to attribute to the evil spirit Ed's call and pushing Ann's "dream button" (paragraph 5). But in accord with the rules I, 2 and 14, it would not be surprising if the evil spirit would take advantage of the situation and try to rush Ann into saying, "Yes, I will." That he was at work is suggested by several following events.

For example, in paragraph 6 we see an evident intense struggle between good and evil spirits. Although her first and most reasonable response had been a firm and unhesitating no, when her "dream button" (from her former rejected mode of life) was pushed, she suddenly lost all recollection of what she had been through and failed to realize the consequences that would flow from giving in to Ed's urging; she found herself saying yes. There seems to be a lack of freedom and rational clarity, a sort of compulsion in this sudden reversal of her decision in opposition to the whole spiritual trend of her life—all this suggesting the influence of the evil spirit. The conflict between this compulsive decision and all the deepest and best dispositions growing within her under the influence of the Holy Spirit very quickly shows itself in the violent physical symptoms and the awareness of the bad consequences to come, culminating in her mentally screaming, What have I done? All this disturbance, leading back to clarity and good sense, indicates the Holy Spirit affecting her in that dimension of her being that was so clearly in conflict with his work in her (rule II, 7).

As soon as these spiritually healthy motions arise in opposition to her regressive decision, she is immediately assailed by thoughts hitherto unfamiliar to her, thoughts plainly bearing the mark of the evil spirit, attacking as they do the value of all that the Holy Spirit has led her to undertake for God's glory in his people, and leading to the loss of spiritual meaning in her life and to despair about doing anything significant for God's service (I, 4). To counteract this attack by the evil spirit, the Holy Spirit inspires Ann's friend and then her daughter to very simply and directly cut through the obfuscation and lies of the evil spirit, thus bringing Ann back to the clarity of mind and consequently to the peace of heart she had before all the turmoil began (I, 2; II, 1).

3. What swayed Ann once again to regard her former decision as God's will for her was all the reasons why she had in the first place let go of her business and begun a new way of life for God, reasons that her friend and her daughter recalled to her mind. Like the earlier decision, this one also she reached by the third Ignatian mode of seeking God's will. Evidently, at the beginning of her conversion, Ann did experience spiritual consolation and attraction to begin a new life (paragraphs 2 and 3); this it was that led her to question the place of her designer business in this new life. But she says nothing to indicate that she employed this kind of evidence to answer her question in either discernment; rather she arrived at her decision by third-time evidence, by weighing the advantages and disadvantages that keeping her business or letting it go would contribute to the greater glory of God.

● *Responses to Questions for Case 2* ●

1. Two mistakes immediately stand out: Marty's decision not to seek counsel from someone wiser than he about spiritual discernment (I, 13) and his thinking that the spiritual consolations during his retreat gave credence to an inclination which came later on, after the retreat was over.

What of his "feeling good" about this inclination to work in the Orient? A series of questions come to mind. A negative answer to any of them would negate the good feelings as any kind of evidence of God's will. First, was Marty indifferent to all but God's will when this inclination came? Was he motivated purely or at least primarily by love for God? If so, was the "feeling good" about work in the Orient a spiritual consolation? If it was, was the attraction simultaneous and integral with the consolation? If it was, how much of this consolation with attraction was there? Enough to be called "plentiful" (*Sp. Ex.*, ¶176)? In any case, did Marty also use the third Ignatian mode of seeking God's will, by gathering and weighing the advantages and disadvantages of each alternative for the glory of God?

2. Worse things might have happened if Marty had chosen the other alternative, or the long-term consequences of his actual decision might be better than those ensuing from the other alternative. How do we know? The general principle is that consequences following from a finalized discernment can neither confirm nor disconfirm its validity—though they might require a new discernment.

3. Yes, it does. Those whose main motivation is their own self-satisfaction are not open to the Holy Spirit, do not fulfill the most important of the two essential conditions for a sound discernment of God's will. While defective discernment can conclude to what is in fact God's will, discerners whose discernments are defective through their own fault cannot have any justifiable assurance that they have found God's will. If, however, the discerners in all good will are doing the best they can, then they can be confident that the Holy Spirit will make up for their blameless weakness.

4. Marty is discerning under a presumably competent director, at least one who has learning and experience far beyond Marty's. Marty is indifferent to all but God's will (paragraph 6). He is using significant information that he had ignored in the earlier discernment, in order to get third-time along with second-time evidence.

• *Responses to Questions for Case 3* •

1. Yes. Neither alternative in paragraphs 1 and 2 is of itself morally commanded or forbidden; both are of themselves (that is, apart from their tension as alternatives in this concrete situation for choice) morally good courses of action, both for the glory of God. The question to be answered is which alternative in the concrete circumstances is for Rebecca the better choice, the one that is more for the glory of God. (Whether choosing the alternative that is less for the glory of God is in this concrete situation morally bad is a question that does not concern us.)

2. Betty (and perhaps the lecturer she heard) failed to note Ignatius's distinction between spiritual and nonspiritual consolation and desolation and the significance of this distinction for analyzing and interpreting Rebecca's affective experiences regarding her alternatives for choice. There is no reason to think that either the consolation or the desolation which Rebecca describes and Betty interprets as evidence of the Holy Spirit or of the evil spirit is anything other than the natural, nonspiritual feelings of someone in love. These feelings and the attraction or aversion arising from them might possibly be of some significance in Ignatian third-time discernment of God's will, but not in the second-time.

3. The consolation in paragraph 3 does not depend on and spring from Rebecca's Christian faith, hope, and charity or in any way lead to an increase of these. Therefore there is no reason to think that the consolation is spiritual or prompted by the Holy Spirit. The experience of desolate feelings at the prospect of abandoning her relationship with Robert does not of itself tend to diminish or destroy her living faith. Hence there is no good reason to judge that the drawing or aversion that accompanies these feelings is prompted by the evil spirit. In paragraphs 4 and 7, however, the consolation seems clearly to be spiritual, arising from living faith; furthermore, that consolation marks as prompted by the Holy Spirit, at least with some probability, the attraction to dedicate her life to the service of Christ in the poor. The desolation, the sense of separation from Christ, felt by Rebecca at the thought of living in affluence with those whose predominant values are wealth and social status is spiritual but not prompted by the evil spirit. It is simply the reverse side of the consolation and drawing of the Holy Spirit to a life in union with the poor and humble Christ. The spiritual consolation and desolation support the same alternative for choice.

4. I would explain to them (Rebecca and Betty) the difference between a discernment directed toward judging which course of action is good and which is evil and a discernment directed toward judging which of two good courses of action is the better, the one that God prefers.

I would explain the essential conditions for successfully carrying out the latter kind of discernment and the fundamentals of the Ignatian modes of discernment, clarifying especially the second mode and using Rebecca's own experiences to illustrate it. (She has already had ample second-time evidence of God calling her to a life dedicated to the service of the poor.) I would show that she now needs to seek God's will regarding further decisions:

1. Whether to serve the poor with Christ while living as a celibate or as a married woman (with a husband who understands and

sympathizes with her call to serve the poor and will support her in responding to it)

2. If to live a celibate life, whether to do so in a religious community or as a single person outside the religious state

3. If the choice is religious life, in which religious community to live that life

I would counsel Rebecca to make her discernment, if possible, while making the Ignatian Spiritual Exercises.

● **Responses to Questions for Case 4** ●

1. There is at least a strong hint in paragraph 1 that Ignatius employed the third mode of discernment as he reached his decision to undertake studies. If he felt *"more* inclined to study," there was another lesser inclination to some second alternative. The evidence supporting the first alternative was third-time evidence, a reason or reasons showing that it would be more for "the help of souls" to do so. There is no hint of any second-time, much less of first-time, evidence.

2. Rules I, 2, 3, and 5, certainly do point to the Holy Spirit as the prompting source of these illuminations and consolations: they seem to have their source in faith and charity. They appear to be like those Ignatius was accustomed to receive at prayer and at Mass. The significant factor is their coming at a time when they interfered with what Ignatius had discerned to be God's will for him—to study—because that would be more for God's glory in his neighbor. This fact alerts us to Rules II, 4 and 5 (which profoundly qualify the application of Rules I, 2, 3, and 5). In those rules of the second set, Ignatius warns us that the evil spirit can begin by prompting holy thoughts and consolations, and then use these to serve his wicked purpose. Unless the middle and end as well as the beginning of the whole experience are good, the whole experience must be suspect as the work of the evil spirit. This Ignatius found to be the case at this time.

3. At first glance, making the supposition of attraction along with and integral with the consolations, these experiences would appear to be solid second-time evidence of God's will that Ignatius give up studies and return to his simpler way of life. However, it is significant that these movements (illuminations, consolations, and attractions) came only when he began to study. This fact suggests a planned interference with what he had earlier discerned as God's will and for that reason makes the movements suspect as prompted by the evil spirit. It would be unwise to accept them as originating from the Holy Spirit unless they

came also at times when they did not hinder study and when they were supported by third-time evidence for changing his earlier decision.

● *Responses to Questions for Case 5* ●

1. Paragraphs 3–5 lead one to think that Perkins saw the alternatives for choice to be, on the one hand, to follow a call of Christian charity to sacrifice his materially successful and satisfying way of life in California and go to share God's word with his suffering black brethren in Mississippi or, on the other hand, to continue his life in California, seeking "the values of the world."

2. The kind of choice involved in Ignatian discernment of God's will is between alternatives none of which are commanded or forbidden. The question is which of these good alternatives is more for God's glory. The alternatives stated above in response to question 1 pose a choice between a good and, as Perkins sees and states it, a bad alternative, "seeking the values of the world." Therefore, these are not alternatives for Ignatian discernment of God's will.

3. One passage in Perkins's account (paragraph 7) seems to indicate that he had reason to doubt whether God was calling him to go to Mississippi to share God's word with the people there. He also had grounds for seeing his way of life in California as a good one, not just seeking the values of the world. He was caring for his family, discovering the riches of the Bible, growing in love for God, giving testimony to others, and sharing with them his joy and strength from Christian faith (paragraphs 1 and 8). All this gives reason for seeing two good alternatives calling for an Ignatian discernment.

4. Paragraphs 2 and 3 seem to offer third-time evidence for saying that God was calling Perkins to help his people in Mississippi. Paragraph 7 suggests third-time evidence against such a judgment. Paragraphs 8–10 could be seen as giving second-time evidence in support of judging that Perkins was being called by God to go to Mississippi. In fact, we could wonder whether paragraph 9 is relating what was a first-time experience. Without the opportunity to ask questions of Perkins and elicit more information, we cannot, drawing upon what is said, form a sure judgment about any first-time or second-time experiences. What is clear and certain is that third-time evidence played some part in bringing Perkins to a decision: he saw how desperately his people in Mississippi needed what he could share with them, and he thought that he could do more for the glory of God in their lives than he could do even by continuing all the good things he had been doing in California.

5. Yes. Perkins's "growing conviction" (paragraph 3) became a "command" (paragraph 8). He clearly had a sense of certainty that he had found God's will; after exerting his very best efforts, he was without fear of resisting God's will by deciding to go to Mississippi (paragraph 11).

● *Responses to Questions for Case 6* ●

1. The question for choice expressed in paragraph 5 of Perkins's account is ambiguously phrased. What he says could mean that, while God had called him to work for his people in Mississippi, the question is whether now God wills that he should stay there and continue that work or that, under the new circumstances, he should take his family back to California. It could also mean what it clearly means in paragraph 7. There the choice is between doing what Perkins takes to be God's known will, to stay and work in Mississippi (even if that meant losing his son Philip) or going against God's will by returning to California in order to save his son's life. Given this clearer expression of how the issue for choice appeared to Perkins, the ambiguous expression in paragraph 5 must be understood in accord with paragraph 7.

2. No, he did not. There is nothing for him to discern. He was already certain that God willed for him to remain where he had been called to serve. The issue for him was only to choose whether he would or would not, in a spirit of faith and obedient love, do God's known will even at the cost of his son's life. This is not a question for discernment.

3. Even granting that Perkins's previous discernment had reached a trustworthy decision and that God had called him to work in Mississippi, we cannot conclude that now, in the profoundly changed circumstances, it is still God's will for him to carry on in the work begun—not unless we assume the immutability of God's will as found through his previous discernment. If Perkins was making that assumption, then I think he was under a grave misunderstanding. For God might call him to begin a work and then call him to let it go. A life of discernment is open to the unexpected and to the need for ever new discernment in the ever changing situations of human life in this world. The real question for Perkins was, therefore, not "God's will or my son," but rather, What is God's will for me now, in this new situation—to continue my work in Mississippi (even if this means losing my son) or to return to California (where I can hope to save my son's life)? The latter question is one that can be brought to Ignatian discernment of God's will. If Perkins did have a first-time experience that gave him an indubitable certitude of God's will in this new situation, then and only then would paragraph 7 makes sense.

4. There is something in the situation that could be interpreted as third-time evidence in support of returning to California as more for the glory of God. After all, his son's life seemed to be at stake—and with it his wife's happiness. Is there also something in this situation that could be regarded as third-time evidence that God willed Perkins to stay in Mississippi even at the risk of Philip's life? I think there is: the high hope of relieving the miserable and inhuman conditions of life among the many people whom Perkins had come to help, of bringing them to a free and humanly decent, dignified life, balanced against the high probability, almost certainty, that the work begun would come to nothing if he left.

● *Responses to Questions for Case 7* ●

1. These dispositions are included in openness to the Holy Spirit: trustful prayer, simplicity of heart (one desire, one love, one choice, elective indifference to all but God's will), freedom from unjustifiable prejudgments.

2. The first experience mentioned in paragraph 3a is dubiously a spiritual consolation. On the basis of available information, Gretchen seems to be in a euphoric state merely because she was praised. If so, then there is no good reason to judge that the experience constituted any second-time evidence for continuing as coordinator of religious education. However, more information should be elicited to see if, perchance, there is some unmentioned spiritual ground for the happy feeling, for example, a sense of God's love and care for her and those she works for. In the other experience related in paragraph 3a, her consolation does seem to be from the Holy Spirit and integral with the drawing. Therefore there is probable reason to think that the drawing is also from the Holy Spirit. But note that the drawing as Gretchen expresses it is not necessarily to continue as coordinator for religious education. Rosalyn should inquire whether Gretchen has provided a fully accurate report, whether her experienced desire was only for the children to grow in understanding of God's love or, rather, was really a drawing for her to continue as coordinator so as to help them grow in this way. If the former, there is no evidence for her choice. If the latter, there is some second-time evidence.

3. Since the depressed feeling mentioned in paragraph 3b appears to have no spiritual ground but was due entirely to nonspiritual influences, there is no reason for seeing any second-time experience here giving evidence of God's will.

4. Neither the sadness nor the gladness mentioned in paragraph 3c is clearly a spiritual experience; and, even if it were, there was no

drawing to either of her alternatives for choice. Therefore, the whole experience seems irrelevant to her discernment of God's will. (Gretchen's experience of empathy with the loneliness and cheerfulness of the old people could turn out to be evidence in a third-time discernment.)

5. After presenting her evaluation of Gretchen's experiences, Rosalyn should encourage Gretchen to continue waiting and praying for second-time evidence. If it seems advisable, she could have Gretchen undertake a third-time discernment concurrently with the second-time one, but she should stress the importance of keeping the two discernments and the two kinds of evidence distinct from each other. Before recommending a third-time discernment, however, the advisor may judge it wise to wait until a second-time discernment leads to a conclusion or until it appears that no conclusion will be forthcoming. One may hope that the third mode of discernment will arrive at a trustworthy conclusion, which will suffice without any second-time discernment or will serve to reinforce the conclusion reached by the latter mode. (What to do if the conclusions reached by the two modes conflict will be considered in the next case.)

● *Responses to Questions for Case 8* ●

1. Besides the dispositions essential for any discernment of God's will, anyone intending to do the third mode of such discernment needs to understand what Ignatius means by a "tranquil time" as the time for doing third-time discernment and why tranquility is necessary for doing it. The discerner also needs to become informed of the relevant data and especially to understand the main norm to be used for interpreting the data as evidence of God's will, that is, the so-called *magis* principle, the "greater glory" principle. According to this principle, whatever indicates that one alternative for choice will probably be more for the glory of God in human lives than the other alternative/alternatives, more for the praise and service of God, is evidence that this alternative is what God wills the discerner to choose. Every alternative must be for the glory of God or it is not a valid alternative for Ignatian discernment; only when one alternative promises to be *more* for God's glory does the discerner have any evidence inclining toward that one. Under different aspects each alternative will appear to be more for God's glory. The discerner should keep some record of the reasons in support of each alternative. Whatever else about this mode of discernment Gretchen needs to know can be explained as occasion calls for it.

2. Concerning Gretchen's reasons given in paragraph 2 of the case for continuing as parish coordinator of religious education, the first reason (2*a*) supports thinking that her work as coordinator has been

and likely will be for the glory of God, even greatly for the glory of God. But the question to be asked is this: Does the reason given in any way support a conclusion that continuing in this work will be *more* for the glory of God than pastoral care for the elderly? Gretchen's first reason does not support such a conclusion. The second reason she gives in support of continuing as coordinator of religious education (2*b*), if true, is a valid reason for thinking this work might be *more* for the glory of God.

Concerning Gretchen's reasons (in paragraph 3*a*) for accepting a position as pastoral minister to the elderly, her first reason indicates that she is very well fitted to work with the elderly, but evidently she is also well fitted for her present work in religious education. Does this reason, then, say anything about which work would be for the *greater* praise and service of God? Gretchen's second reason for choosing pastoral ministry to the elderly (the fact that she will find this work more satisfying) is not relevant unless her greater satisfaction gives reason to think that she will do more for the glory of God in that work than in the other. She gives no indication that this is the case. Her third reason (3*c*) coalesces with the second and, again, gives no indication that this ministry to the elderly would be more for the praise and service of God.

3. We can hope that Gretchen now has a better understanding of what constitutes evidence of God's will regarding the choice she has to make. Since she does not yet have sufficient evidence for either alternative to justify a trustworthy decision, she should be advised to continue in prayer and in the search for evidence of God's will, trusting that in his time and in his way he will lead her to the right decision. It would be well to remind her that, while she must do her very best, her ultimate trust is not in her own efforts but in the loving guidance of the Holy Spirit. If time runs out and she has to make a decision without any more delay, she may decide as seems better, making use of whatever evidence she has and confidently trusting the Holy Spirit to guide her choice toward God's greater glory in her life and the lives of those she serves.

4. She should weigh the strength of evidence for each conclusion. If the case for one is strong and the other weak, she should go with the strong one. If the two cases are of about equal value, one only slightly stronger, she should pray for help and keep looking for evidence in both modes of discernment. If time runs out and she has to make a decision now (not to do so would be a decision), then, after seeking counsel insofar as possible, she should trust God and follow whichever conclusion seems to her in any way more strongly supported by evidence.

5. She still needs to seek confirmation insofar as time and energy make this possible. What this involves will be studied in a later case.

● *Responses to Questions for Case 9* ●

1. This question cannot be answered with certainty. It is possible that the companions had all discerned well while Ignatius had failed to do so—perhaps failed to be indifferent. It is also possible that Ignatius had made a sound discernment, whereas the companions failed to do so—perhaps they approached to discernment with their minds made up beforehand. It is even possible that they all failed to discern well. But none of these possibilities seems likely, and there is no good reason to assume any of them in order to make sense of what happened.

The question to be discerned by each of the companions, including Ignatius, was not which of them God willed to be general of the Society of Jesus, but only for whom did God will each to cast his vote. He might direct others to vote differently or move the one elected to refuse the office, as Ignatius, in fact, did. Ignatius's refusal could also be the result of a good discernment, for which the issue could not be whether God willed him to be the general but whether God willed him to accept or refuse the result of the preceding election and request a new election.

When the companions did hold another election issuing in the same result and when they now saw a refusal by Ignatius as standing in the way of God's will, Ignatius faced a new situation, calling on him to enter upon a new discernment. However, Ignatius could not see any new evidence for thinking God wanted him to accept the office (other than the result of a second election), so it seemed best to him to entrust discernment to some trustworthy person who was not involved in the issue except for being concerned for the glory of God in Ignatius and the others. Such a one was Ignatius's confessor, Fr. Theodosio.

The judgment reached by Theodosio showed Ignatius what God *now* willed Ignatius to do. It did not imply that Ignatius in his earlier discernment failed to find and resisted God's will for him *at that time*— no more than a contrary judgment by Theodosio would have implied that the companions had failed to find God's will for them (how God wanted each of them to vote, not what God wanted Ignatius to do). God could very well have led (and presumably did lead) Ignatius and the companions to their decisions, which were answers to different questions, not contradictory answers to the same questions—though the answers did entail conflicting practical consequences.

If, after Theodosio had done all that Ignatius had requested, Ignatius still stubbornly refused the election, the companions and Theodosio might with reason have accused him of resisting the Holy Spirit.

2. There is nothing in the narrative to suggest any mode of election other than the third. Reasons that he interpreted as demonstrating his unsuitability for the office clearly led Ignatius to his refusal. The whole tenor of the narrative indicates that Theodosio's discernment was based on an evaluation of the reasons which Ignatius (and, presumably, the companions) supplied. If the discernments by Ignatius and Theodosio brought into play any second-time evidence, nothing is said about it. Certainly Ignatius showed no sign of any attraction with spiritual consolation when he gave in and accepted his election.

● *Response to Question for Case 10* ●

To answer this question, we need to be clear about the kind of discernment Jack Black can make. If he understands the kind of discernment of God's will that he is able to make in this situation, then he will see that there can be no contradiction between the conclusion of his discernment and that of Howard White, for they are answering different questions. Jack Black has, by his vow of obedience in the Society of Jesus, renounced the right and responsibility to choose his own ministry; he has given that right and responsibility to the Society of Jesus and to the provincial who exercises executive authority in that Society. What he does have in this situation is the right and the responsibility to make a *consultative* discernment and thus provide input for the provincial's *deliberative* discernment. The question that he should seek to answer in his discernment is not, Does God will me to be the new local superior? It is, rather, Does God want me to advise for or against the proposed appointment? On the other hand, the question that the provincial should seek to answer in his deliberative discernment is, Does God will me to appoint Jack Black as the local superior? (More precisely, Does God will that I efficaciously intend to appoint . . . ?) In seeking the answer to that question, he has a responsibility to give serious consideration to Jack Black's advice and his evidence for it; he has no responsibility to conform to Jack Black's advice.

● *Response to Question for Case 11* ●

Jack Black has learned well from his previous experience; but he still needs to learn that besides deliberative and consultative discernment of God's will, there is another type that can be called delegated or entrusted discernment. This latter type differs from consultative discernment in that the one who has the right and responsibility to make a choice in a given matter but who delegates another to enter into discernment regarding this matter has already chosen in principle whatever his delegate will discern. This mode of discerning is reasonable and trustworthy only when the one delegating has done his or her reasonable best without success or when it is clear to her or him that another person or group is definitely in a better position to discern God's will in this situation and can be trusted to do so.

Ignatius was emphatically of the opinion that in general those who were actually in the concrete situation calling for a decision were better able to discern God's will than was a faraway superior. For that reason he encouraged local superiors to make their own decisions (discerningly, of course) and, if it seemed worth doing so, to keep him informed afterwards. In accord with this attitude, on at least one occasion he acted exactly as did Fr. Sansouci.

If, however, Fr. Sansouci (or Ignatius) could, without unreasonable delay, devote the time and energy required to master the details of the situation and thus be in as good a position to discern God's will as the local community and if it was reasonable for him to invest the time and effort, then one could well argue that he was avoiding his responsibility and invalidly delegating discernment to the community.

• *Responses to Questions for Case 12* •

1. Although it is possible that what serves as intellectual confirmation of a conclusion can also serve as volitional confirmation, the two are always formally, even if not materially, distinct. Intellectual confirmation in the context of discerning God's will is confirmation of a conclusion reached by spiritual discernment of God's will and is constituted by evidence that God approves the decision, that it truly expresses what God wills the discerner to choose. It is concerned with the truth of a judgment. Volitional confirmation is not evidence regarding a judgment made or to be made: it is a strengthening of the discerners' resolve to choose an action in accord with the conclusion reached and to carry out the chosen action against obstacles from within or without. When the decision, the judgment about what God wills, is as yet tentative, the discerner looks for intellectual confirmation, evidence to strengthen the conviction of the truth of this judgment and to justify finalizing it. When the concluding judgment is finalized, the discerner needs volitional confirmation, encouragement to stiffen resolve to carry through what has been judged to be God's will. If Richard's conclusion in his discernment was not yet finalized, as seems to have been the case, then the confirmation he needed and did not get was intellectual.

When his conclusion was in fact disconfirmed by second-time evidence (attraction in spiritual consolation), leading him to finalize a different conclusion, the same kind of evidence that constituted intellectual confirmation served also as volitional confirmation.

2. Lack of confirming evidence for the tentative decision when discerning God's will is not a disconfirmation of the judgment reached. In fact, if a judgment is reached by a sound discernment with trustworthy evidence, the silence of God when confirmation is sought can be interpreted as approval. For, once discernment has been carried out to the best of the discerner's ability in the concrete situation, it is up to God to disconfirm the conclusion by clearer evidence if it is wrong. If God does not disconfirm it, the discerner can reasonably judge that he accepts it. In other words, God's silence in this situation is a tacit confirmation.

3. The answer is negative. Since the decision is only tentative and the discerner is still seeking confirmation before finalizing it, a disconfirmation is only another step in the process leading toward a different conclusion or decision. As Richard points out in his narration (paragraph 4), it was by the disconfirmation of what he calls a "wrong decision" that God in his providence led him to the right decision, which he (Richard) might otherwise have avoided.

4. What justifiably called into question the trustworthiness of Richard's decision was his failure to reach true elective indifference toward one of the alternatives. This failure rendered his discernment defective and its conclusion untrustworthy. This is not the same as disconfirming the conclusion. He might have reached a true conclusion even by a defective discernment; but he would not be justified in trusting that he had done so. To reach a trustworthy conclusion, he would have to become truly indifferent and then make a new discernment.

5. To demand total freedom from any spontaneous inclination to every one of the alternatives for choice when seeking God's will would be unrealistic. Sometimes such freedom is an ideal disposition for discerning God's will; but frequently, in the concrete, even with the greatest goodwill it is beyond the person's power. What is more, it is sometimes not even an ideal. For being totally free of some spontaneous inclinations would be psychologically and morally an unhealthy condition. Those who felt no aversion to doing what would cause pain to others or require separation from their friends would be emotionally and morally insensitive. What is required to adequately fulfill the indifference required for discerning God's will is a disposition constituted by a love for God and desire for his glory in the world so strong that any natural inclination would not only be unable to sway the discerners

from choosing God's known preferential will but even be unable to influence their judgment, blinding them to what is God's preferential will and begetting judgments by a selfish affective connaturality. In short, what constitutes the indifference required for seeking God's will is a love for God with a desire for his glory so strong as to render any opposing love and desire powerless to affect the discerners' reason and judgment.

6. If this turn of events had taken place, it would have said nothing to disconfirm Richard's decision. To understand why this is so requires a precise understanding of the limits of discerning God's will. The truth is that, without the gift of prophesying future events, it is impossible for Richard (or anyone else) to discern whether or not God actually wills him to become a Jesuit or to get married or to do anything else. In fact, Richard could not even discern whether God willed for him to be accepted into the novitiate. All anyone can discern about God's will is what God prefers that he choose here and now to efficaciously intend to do. By an efficacious intention I mean one that will be effective when the opportunity for appropriately executing it is presented and will persist in the future until the person sees that God now wills for him to change it. So whether Richard understood it or not, all that he could really have discerned was that God willed for him to efficaciously intend to apply to the Jesuits and become one if that would be God's will in the future. Even when this limit of discerning God's will is understood and accepted, we will no doubt go on formulating our questions for discernment of God's will in the imprecise and misleading way that we do; but we can avoid being misled if we keep in mind what has just been pointed out. So, in a direct answer to the question asked, if after being accepted into the novitiate, Richard later on found that he could not live as a Jesuit and discerned that God now willed for him to leave the novitiate (to efficaciously intend to leave), that would in no way indicate that his earlier discernment was defective or its conclusion untrue. He should, rather, think that God, for his kind purpose, wanted him in the novitiate for as long as he was.

●   *Responses to Questions for Case 13*   ●

1. Without any more precise information than what is given, I would see a real possibility that the discerner might fall into error by adding to what was in experiences he had and on which he based his decision. He might have added something to the inspiration from the Holy Spirit during spiritual consolation. He speaks of an "inspiration one day to give himself wholly" to God. But that is the vocation of every Christian in every state of life. It is true that when he recalled the times

of desolation with temptation against this inspiration (paragraph 2), there is an indication that the inspiration was to the religious state of life. But life as a Jesuit is only one among a large number of ways of leading the religious life.

2. In the case under consideration, it would be necessary to question the discerner in order to find out whether the experience of drawing, of "inspiration," that came during the spiritual consolation was merely a drawing to give himself wholly to God or whether the inspiration was more specifically an inspiration to give himself to God in the religious state of life and, if so, whether it was even more specifically toward becoming a Jesuit. If the inspiration was not that specific, then he has been adding to the inspiration of the Holy Spirit; and his evidence is not evidence of a call to be a Jesuit or, perhaps, even to be a religious of any kind. This leaves open the possibility that he is being deceived, that God's will might be for him to be a Franciscan, a Carthusian, or a member of any other religious order—or that he give himself wholly to God's service in the lay state of life, married or celibate.

3. Yes, these experiences of spiritual desolation along with aversion to religious life are significant. By themselves they would be of little help for finding whether God willed for this young man to live in a religious state. If the attractions during spiritual consolations were toward the religious state, however, then the aversion to that state that came during spiritual desolation would be helpful evidence. The reason is that, just as spiritual consolation is a sign of the Holy Spirit influencing us, so also spiritual desolation is a sign of the evil spirit influencing our affectivity and thoughts. We can reasonably assume that what the evil spirit suggests is opposed to God's will and that the contradictory or contrary of it is God's will. Consequently, the experiences of aversion in spiritual desolation will strengthen the evidence from the drawing during spiritual consolation.

4. I would first advise him to make sure he is in an attitude of indifference, as far as possible and suitable having no inclination to any alternative for choice except insofar as it appears to be God's will and admitting no motive for choosing any alternative except because God wills it. When confident of having that attitude, he should reflect on the second-time experiences that he has already had to see how they are to be interpreted and, if need be, wait and pray for more definite guidance. Along with this second-time discernment, he should also make a third-time discernment of God's will to see whether weighing each alternative's advantages and disadvantages for the greater glory of God leads to a conclusion that agrees with the conclusion based on second-time evidence or if it tends to oppose the latter conclusion. Discernment

by the second mode of seeking God's will (through consolations with attraction) can be sufficient by itself; but if the discerner has the time and energy to seek God's will by the third mode also, doing one's best calls for doing that. Ignatius's own practice was to do so. When a tentative decision has been reached, the discerner should seek confirmation. When the decision is finalized, the discerner should give thanks to God and act on the decision promptly.

• *Responses to Questions for Case 14* •

1. It would be necessary to question Victor to learn whether the consolations he experienced were truly spiritual ones; if so, whether they were prompted by the Holy Spirit; and whether the attractions he felt were during the consolations and integral with them. Unless the answers to all these questions are affirmative, the experiences are not genuine second-time experiences and are not evidence for finding God's will by the second mode of discernment.

If the experiences are truly second-time experiences, then it will be necessary to question Victor about what it was to which he was attracted. Was the attraction he experienced in spiritual consolation more precise than he has indicated? Was there any drawing to a particular mode of religious life—to a purely contemplative way of life or to a mixed way of life, contemplative and active? If so, to which particular community of that mode? If the attraction was to no more than religious life in general, then Victor has more discernment to do. If it was for a particular community in a particular mode of religious life and the second-time evidence was sufficient for a tentative decision, then it might still be advisable for him to make a third-time discernment before seeking confirmation. This would be called for if he is to make his best effort.

2. There seems to be, in paragraph 4, a hint of a first-time experience. If Victor did have such an experience, it would explain several obscurities in this paragraph that paragraphs 1–3 do nothing to clarify. It would explain why the desire for religious life "never for an instant" left him; why memories of joy in his family and in a secular life had not at all troubled him; and, above all, why, even though the preceding reasons he gave by no means justify complete and unshakable certainty, he says, "I *cannot doubt* that God calls me to the religious life because his holy will is too plainly manifest" (emphasis mine).

3. The answers to these questions depend on how we interpret what Ignatius says about the first time. All agree that the first-time experience includes an indubitable judgment of what the subject is called to and of the fact that it is God who calls. According to one

interpretation this certainty is such that the experience neither needs nor allows for any reflective critical evaluation. A second interpretation sees the whole experience, including the unshakable certainty, as data for reflection. In terms of this latter interpretation, the unreflective certainty needs to be reflected on in order to evaluate it critically, to reach a reflective judgment that the experience is a genuine first-time experience, and to make sure to what the subject is being drawn. In a parallel way, the first interpretation makes any second-time or third-time evidence useless, whereas the second interpretation can use these kinds of evidence as a way of critically evaluating the unreflective first-time experience.

● *Responses to Questions for Case 15* ●

1. Yes. Paragraphs 2–5 and 8 show that Tonya did her best to carry through the process of praying, gathering information, seeking counsel, reasoning on the data with a sincere intention of finding and doing God's will, all the while holding herself indifferent to all but God's will, indifferent even to living or dying.

2. As seen in the practice of St. Ignatius, signs for the time to conclude a search for God's will are present when Tonya brings her discernment to a close: a sense of having accomplished, under God's guidance, all she reasonably could and a sense of confidence that what she decided was truly what God willed (see paragraph 6).

3. We have already seen that Tonya's discernment seems to be sound and the conclusion trustworthy (see response 2, question 1). It is possible that the Maryknoll superior failed to discern or discern well and came to a decision in conflict with God's will. It is also possible that the superior did find God's will and it was for him or her to tell Tonya she could not go to Guatemala. The superior and Tonya could both have found God's will. How this could be is not, as in some previous cases we have studied, cleared up by saying that Tonya's discernment was merely consultative. As Tonya herself sees, in paragraph 9, the answer to our question depends on understanding the limits of discerning God's will. Tonya could not discern that God intended her to actually go to Guatemala. To know that would require a gift of prophesying the future. She could discern what God, at the precise time when she concluded her discernment, wanted her to efficaciously intend to do, namely, to go to Guatemala—and, even though she did not know it, that was all she could discern. Such an intention could be frustrated without invalidating the conclusion of her discernment. Through all that happened God was governing the situation and giving Tonya the grace to grow in faith and love and trust.

• *Responses to Questions for Case 16* •

1. I would guess that Father Albert had a first-time experience. There is no evidence in his story of any second-time or third-time evidence leading him to his decision. He just seems to experience a sudden reversal of the attitude expressed to his superior a little while before and a certainty that such was God's will for him. If Father Albert did not come to his decision by a first-time experience, then I would guess that it was by the third Ignatian mode, one of those deliberations which happen in a moment, when manifold evidence comes together and yields a clear conclusion that resembles an intuition. There is no indication of a decision by the second Ignatian mode of election.

2. I would ask whether he had experienced a powerful attraction with certitude that the attraction was from God, whether the certitude was so firm that he could not doubt even if he tried. If Father Albert's answer to these questions should be negative, I would exclude the first mode of finding God's will and take a different tack. I would ask him to outline for me what went on in his mind and led up to his surprising conviction that God wanted him to go as a missionary to Jamaica—and I would await his answer with intense curiosity.

3. I would explain to Father Albert (if he needed explanation) what constitutes the indifference requisite for discerning God's will and why such indifference is requisite. I would advise him to examine his attitude and, if he had not arrived at the requisite indifference, urge him to pray for a pure heart. I would recommend as well that he hold off not only his response to his superior but even a tentative decision until he was confident he was truly indifferent to any alternative for God's service except insofar as it might be God's will for him.

When he had achieved that attitude, I would point out to him that his discernment could be only consultative, and would then explain (if there was need for explanation) the three modes of seeking God's will and reflect with him on the decision arrived at on the subway, trying to determine which mode it was. If it seemed to him to be the first mode, I would advise him to try to doubt it. If he could not, I would tell him that such an experience is enough to act on, but would go on to suggest that if he reasonably could, it would be well to see what came from a second-time (if God made it possible) and a third-time discernment.

When all the evidence was in and a decision finalized, I would urge Father Albert to give thanks to God and act on his decision promptly, especially if it should be one to which he had a natural aversion.

●   *Responses to Questions for Case 17*   ●

1.   Jenny is being attacked by spiritual desolations: she has experiences of distress and confusion that attack faith, hope, and charity and tend to discourage her. It is the evil spirit who prompts these experiences (I, 2, 4f.; II, 7). On the other hand, she occasionally experiences the consolation of the Holy Spirit—spiritual peace, courage, and energy to persevere in striving (I, 2, 3, 5). In short, Jenny's mind and heart are a battleground for spiritual and antispiritual forces, as is to be expected when anyone seriously sets about striving to live the Christian life more fully. The evil spirit afflicts persons such as Jenny, trying to hinder their spiritual growth. God allows the power of darkness to do this for those persons' good (I, 9); and, while persons so afflicted feel at times as though God has deserted them and all is lost, the truth is that God is always with them, giving them strength to overcome all the attacks of evil (I, 7). With confidence in God's care and power, no matter how Jenny feels, she will be able to continue seeking help from a capable spiritual director and persevering generously in prayer and work. If she does, she will by God's power overcome all present and future attacks (I, 11).

2.   One who has no understanding of the spiritual experiences that Ignatius deals with in his rules or of how to interpret them in discerning God's will might see Jenny's emotional difficulties as strong evidence that she is out of her element in religious life. In the light of Ignatius's teaching, however, there is nothing in this account which can reasonably be viewed as third-time evidence that Jenny has made a mistake in coming to the religious community and should now leave it. If Jenny's difficulties clearly sprang from bad will or from psychological incapacity to live in a religious community, what she is experiencing could be understood as some evidence (not necessarily conclusive) that she should leave—if and only if that seemed good to her when she was calm or in spiritual consolation. Desolation is no time to change previously well made decisions. But the facts are that she seems to manifest great goodwill, a courageous, generous spirit, and the ability to get along with others and work effectively.

Neither is there any second-time evidence that could reasonably be interpreted as evidence of God's will for Jenny to leave the religious community. Rather, there is repeated second-time evidence that God wants her where she is: whenever she experiences spiritual consolation, she feels certain of God's call to persevere in religious life and feels inclined to do so. Furthermore, her negative moods are not just psychological depression but rather spiritual desolation; when in spiritual desolation, she appears inclined to give up and leave the community.

All this strengthens rather than weakens the second-time evidence regarding God's will. These inclinations during spiritual desolation are presumably from the evil spirit and, therefore, counterindicative of God's will.

• *Responses to Questions for Case 18* •

1. Helen is primarily a spiritually maturing woman, being led by the Holy Spirit but revealing at least one obvious disposition opposed to the work of the Holy Spirit, a certain selfish desire to be important in the church's work, to have status in the parish.

2. All or almost all of the rules in the first set would apply, and consideration of them would help Helen. The evil spirit is active in putting obstacles in the way of those who, like Helen, are striving to serve God (I, 2; II, 7). Her change of feelings about involving others in the work and eventually her sense of God's absence bear the marks of spiritual desolation and temptation prompted by the evil spirit (I, 4). In such a state she should not deliberate about making a new decision, that is, about giving up her work (I, 5). Her failure to take counsel with a competent guide was playing into the hands of the evil spirit (I, 13), and her reason for not consulting another shows a patent absence of indifference to all but God's will. The enemy has discovered weak points, her self-interest in doing work for God, the weakness that accounts for her feeling of insecurity and resentment (I, 14). She did not oppose the evil spirit promptly and strongly (I, 12). She needed to change her attitude and to do whatever could help her to do so (I, 6). One help would be to consider why she finds herself in spiritual desolation (I, 9). Through all this time, she needs to remember with faith that God is always with her even when he seems faraway (I, 7) and to trust that he will soon relieve her desolation (I, 8).

3. At first glance, it seems clear that the Holy Spirit was prompting spiritual consolation (I, 3). However, it is possible that the evil spirit was acting as an angel of light, prompting spiritual consolation in order later to deceive Helen into a well-meant but wrong decision (II, 3–5). There is need to evaluate this experience critically. (See response to question 4.)

4. It is dubious whether Helen has any sound evidence for such a decision as God's will. There are many questions to ask in order to evaluate it. Was the consolation truly spiritual? If not, then it cannot be evidence supporting her decision. If so, was the consolation prompted by the Holy Spirit or by the evil spirit? The answer to this question would involve, among other things, determining whether Helen's retirement would contribute more or less to God's service. If the Holy Spirit

prompted the consolation, did the attraction to retire come at the same time and was it integral with the spiritual consolation? If not, the experience has no value as evidence. If the drawing was integral with spiritual consolation, is one such experience sufficient to justify so serious a decision?

After such questioning, I would counsel Helen that, if the idea of retiring perseveres, she should make a formal Ignatian discernment about it, looking for more plentiful and more certain evidence through attraction in spiritual consolation; she should also make a third-time discernment, looking for sound reasons for or against staying with the work she was doing for the glory of God. Do stronger reasons exist for retiring or for staying?

● *Responses to Questions for Case 19* ●

1. There is evidence that David's intending to become a priest and taking steps toward that end are a real alternative for his discernment of God's will. His character and way of life in the service of God's people show he is qualified for that role in the Church and the insistent drawing toward the priesthood suggests a call from the Holy Spirit. But none of this by itself is evidence that God is actually calling him to the priesthood. David needs some sign that the drawing is from the Holy Spirit and not from some other source. He needs evidence that as a priest he could be and do more for the glory of God than he could in his present way of life or in some other way.

2. Yes, his powerful experience of God as described in paragraph 6 revealed to him, among other things, his lack of what Ignatius speaks of as indifference to all but God's will: he saw that he had been coming at his decision making principally in terms of what he would like to do for God instead of concerning himself only or at least primarily with what God willed for him to do. This could be a cause of insensitivity to movements of the Holy Spirit, accounting for David's consequent unclarity and vacillation. Also in the whole account, David fails to go about his discernment in an orderly way, with clear norms to guide his search. His discernment might have proceeded with less confusion if he had been guided through a methodical process such as Ignatius proposes in the *Spiritual Exercises*. Not that such a method precludes all uncertainty and wavering or automatically effects a sure conclusion; but it does help greatly to keep the discernment on track, remove obstacles, and keep the discerner open to divine guidance.

3. Understanding and applying rules 1, 2, 4, 5, and 9, would help David to understand what is happening in his prayer and why it is happening. (The person using this book to learn Ignatian discernment

would do well to go through these rules reflectively and consider how they would apply to David.)

4. The needed counsels are included in rules I, 4–8, 12. The rules would show David how to deal with the spiritual desolation he is experiencing so as to grow spiritually through it rather than suffer harm. (Again, as in the response to question 3, the reader would do well to reflect on these rules and consider how they apply to David's experience.)

5. The experience related in paragraph 6 seems to be what Ignatius, in rule II, 2, names a "consolation without preceding cause." The possible function of this kind of spiritual consolation in finding God's will and counsel on how to guard against possible deception in connection with it are treated in rule II, 8. However, since in paragraph 6 David does not mention that attraction to or aversion from the priesthood is joined with the consolation, this later rule does not apply here.

What did come with and is a result of the consolation was David's keen awareness of the attitude with which he had been approaching discernment, an attitude in conflict with a fundamental condition essential to sound discernment. (See above, the response to question 2.)

6. Along with rules I, 2 and 5, which we considered above in the response to question 3, rule I, 3 (Ignatius's description of spiritual consolation) applies here. For David was surely experiencing spiritual consolation as high as his desolation (paragraph 3) had been deep, a consolation rooted in his intensified faith in God's love for him, his "whole life . . . radically changed" by it. This phrase, "whole life . . . radically changed," I take to refer, not or not only to his sadness changed into joy, but to the reversal of his concern for what *he* wanted to a concern for what *God* wanted. Rules I, 10 and 11, supply relevant counsels on how to deal with spiritual consolation so as not to misuse it, but to let it work God's intention in giving it.

7. Yes, the experience as David describes it could readily suggest that he was experiencing what Ignatius calls the first time for finding God's will, a drawing without being able to doubt that the drawing is from God and reveals God's will for him. If it was not a first-time experience, then it was a second-time experience, a drawing integral with spiritual consolation but without eliminating the power of doubting that God is drawing him. If it is a second-time experience, then what happened at this time is evidence regarding God's will but by itself insufficient: "plentiful light" from signs of this sort is needed to justify a trustworthy conclusion.

8. It seems clear that David was in need of some basic instruction on the essential conditions for a trustworthy discernment of God's will

and on the kinds of evidence of it that he should seek. The latter would require clarifying the *magis* principle (the greater-glory principle) employed in the third mode of election, the meaning of spiritual consolation and desolation, and their significance for discerning God's will in the second mode. Along with all this information, David would need some basic instruction on how to proceed in seeking and recording evidence. More detailed instruction on how to proceed and to discern spirits would best be brought up as David's experiences made it needful.

● *Responses to Questions for Case 20* ●

1. It is only the third mode for which this case offers any evidence. Francis gathered the reasons pro and con for each alternative and weighed the reasons for one against those for the other. There is no suggestion of any second-time evidence.

2. Here also there is no indication of any mode of discernment except what Ignatius calls the third mode. The only evidence Clare and Silvester gave to Francis to bolster their answer was a reason, namely, that God did not call him only for his own sake but for the sake of many others to be helped by him. Again, there is no suggestion of second-time evidence leading them to their conclusion.

3. I think it was a delegated discernment. It seems clear from what went before and after Clare and Silvester had made their discernments. Francis could not find the answer for himself, so he sent Masseo to ask Clare and Silvester to find what God wanted him to do, not merely to offer some counsel that would be helpful in his own discernment. Most significant is the fact that when Francis received their answer, he immediately took this to be God's will; and without any further deliberation or search for signs from God, he acted on it.

4. Yes, I think Francis was justified. He seems to have tried his best but was unable to reach the decision on his own, and those to whom he entrusted the discernment were persons altogether worthy of trust to find what God willed for him to do.

● *Responses to Questions for Case 21* ●

1. Eileen admits that the reasons given by her friends (paragraph 2) have validity (paragraph 3), and are, therefore, her own reasons for regarding her appointment as novice director as God's will. It seems to me, however, that all these reasons do no more by themselves than show that Eileen is adequate for the proposed assignment. They do nothing to address whether being novice director would be more for the service of God than her work at the university. Consequently, the rea-

sons are not yet satisfactorily formulated. Every such reason must show not merely that an alternative is for God's glory or that it is a real alternative for the discerner's choice, one she can reasonably undertake; such considerations are prerequisite for any proposed course of action to be a valid alternative for a discernment of God's will. What any reason must show if it is to be relevant is that one alternative will likely be in some respect *more* for the glory of God than the other alternative.

2. In paragraph 4 Eileen lists her reasons for a negative response, her deficiency in many areas of knowledge and her need to learn more in order to be properly prepared for the position of novice director. Again, however, all that these reasons show is that Eileen is not as fully prepared as she would like to be, not that, in the concrete situation, it would be more for the service and glory of God if she were not appointed; much less do these reasons show that her continuing in academic work would likely be a greater service to God.

3. On the basis of what is presented as evidence, I would say that, on the one hand, the reasons for an affirmative response, if better formulated, could make a cogent case. On the other hand, Eileen's alleged need for more preparation does validly argue against an affirmative response. However, the actual situation is the key point. The question is not whether, apart from this situation, it would be better for the provincial to appoint someone else; the question is, rather, whether Eileen is already able to do at least an adequate job and is better suited than any other person available in the community. In answer to this question, in the concrete situation the evidence that Eileen should accept the appointment seems clearly stronger—unless some other factor not yet mentioned enters the picture to show it to be more for God's service and glory that she remain in university work. Here lies the weakness of the whole deliberation: Nothing is clearly said about the comparative values of the two alternatives, about which one would be better than the other for God's glory in the community, in the people they work for, and in Eileen herself. This is not a good example of how to go about a third-time discernment of God's will.

4. Eileen seems to be appealing to another kind of evidence, what Ignatius calls second-time evidence. This is evidence for answering the question, To what alternative is God drawing me? (as distinct from the question, Which alternative appears to be more for the service and glory of God?). If so, before evaluating what she adduces as evidence, we must respond to a number of questions.

First, attraction to one of the alternatives along with peace and joy constitutes this kind of evidence; but the attraction and the peace and joy are all of a special kind. The attraction that counts in this mode of discerning God's will is *not* attraction to this alternative as something I would enjoy doing, but as something that God wills. The peace and joy that count are not peace and joy at the thought of doing what I like and enjoy doing. The peace and joy, the consolation, are *spiritual;* that is, they are rooted in religious faith, love, and hope, the work of the Holy Spirit in us. Are Eileen's attraction and her peace and joy the kind that count? Further, only when the attraction to one alternative comes at the same time as spiritual consolation and is integral with it is there any evidence for what God wills. Is this the case with Eileen's attraction with consolation?

It is not at all clear that Eileen understands what constitutes evidence for the second mode of discerning God's will. Even if she does, there is in paragraph 5 an implication that second-time evidence is necessary for any trustworthy discernment of God's will and that the lack of it in support of an alternative is decisive evidence that this alternative is not God's will. This way of thinking is certainly in conflict with the teaching of St. Ignatius. In his thought, second-time evidence, evidence by drawing in spiritual consolation, is *one* very important way of finding God's will, but is not *the* way. The absence of such affirmative evidence does not at all constitute decisive negative evidence. In fact, it is not evidence of anything except that the discerner is to seek God's will by the third mode.

5. Eileen's negative feelings at the thought of discontinuing her work in the university, losing tenure, and leaving unfinished her book in progress indicate a serious lack of openness to the Holy Spirit, a failure to reach "indifference to all but God's will." Being troubled, discouraged, and resentful does not reveal an attitude of concern that is wholly or at least primarily for the greater glory of God. These feelings are signs of egocentric concern and the influence of the evil spirit rather than signs of the Holy Spirit moving her to continue her present work.

6. Without clarifications in accord with what was said above in response to question 4, the experience referred to in paragraph 6 remains altogether too ambiguous to be of any help. It would be necessary to question Eileen carefully about it, in order to interpret her experience and see its value for finding God's will.

7. In order to make a trustworthy discernment on the immediate question regarding the proposed assignment, Eileen needs, above all else, to become more open to the Holy Spirit than she is thus far, to have an attitude of genuine indifference in the Ignatian meaning of that term in the context of Christian decision making. She also needs to make this discernment under the direction of some capable director

who is learned and experienced in discernment of spirits and discernment of God's will.

8. In the long run, Eiieen needs to become aware of her ignorance about discernment of spirits and of God's will and to do some serious study of these matters. What she says shows that as yet she does not accurately understand what constitutes either second-time or third-time evidence of God's will.

• *Responses to Questions for Case 22* •

1. The experience as Charles describes it appears to be without any mediation by his own thoughts, images, feelings, or volitions. Does it, then, describe what Ignatius names a "consolation without previous cause"? Not every spiritual experience without previous cause is a consolation, and Charles says of this one, "There was no warmth, no notable consolation, just an assurance that I had made the right choice."

Was the experience, then, what Ignatius names a first time or occasion for an election, that is, "a time when God our Lord so moves and draws the will that, without doubting or the power of doubting, the faithful person follows what is shown" (*Sp. Ex.*, ¶175)? The experience does have elements that would suggest a first-time experience. Something is shown without any gathering of evidence, without any process to establish it. With this message is given a strong certainty. Whether this certainty was, as it is in a first-time experience, such that Charles could not doubt even if he tried, we do not know. In any case, however, Charles did not experience a "first time for election"; for no matter how he might have reached his decision, the decision had already been made. In this experience there was, he says, no call; he received a confirmation that the decision he had already made was the right one, the one in accord with God's will. The confirmation was primarily and obviously an intellectual confirmation, but very likely also a volitional confirmation, strengthening his resolve to execute his right decision. It would not, it seems to me, be wrong to say that Charles was given a confirmation without previous cause or a confirmation by a quasi first-time experience.

A comment is in order here. In *Discerning God's Will*, chapters 11 and 12, I discussed confirmation before finalizing a decision, and I rejected as invalid several common ways of looking for intellectual confirmation *after* finalizing the decision. In those chapters I wrote nothing about the ways in which a finalized decision can be intellectually as well as volitionally confirmed. This regrettable omission might lead the reader to think that there can be no intellectual confirmation after finalizing a decision but only volitional confirmation. As this case shows, such a way of thinking would be mistaken.

● *Responses for Case 23* ●

1. The drawing is something good and comes during spiritual consolation. Therefore, at first glance, it seems to be from God (rules I, 2, 3, and 5). However, as Ignatius warns in rule II, Patrick needs to be alert for any sign of a deception prompted by the evil spirit. As our study of this case proceeds, we too must be alert in the same way.

2. These experiences seem to be what Ignatius, in rule II, 2, of his Rules for Discernment of Spirits, calls consolation without previous cause. Since God alone, according to Ignatius, can cause, prompt, such consolation, it cannot entail any deception. However, he sees a danger that the one who receives consolation without previous cause can be deceived by purposes and opinions which come *immediately after* the actual consolation, during its afterglow. This afterglow can be distinguished from any actual consolation only by alert and careful reflective attention. Any drawing or plan that comes during the afterglow is subject to the same deceptions as any drawing or plan that comes during consolation with previous cause and must be put to the same tests. Further, as Ignatius stresses in his well-known letter to Teresa Rejadell, the drawing or plan which comes during a spiritual consolation must be carefully reflected on to make sure that it is remembered *exactly* as it came *at the time* of the consolation, *without addition or subtraction.*

3. The information gathered here confirms that Patrick has been and is faithful to his present way of life, that he is neither merely discontented and looking for a change nor hindered by his present way of life from growth into union with God nor unfit for active ministry. Rather, he has been peacefully growing in union with God and working fruitfully in his ministry. Therefore, the burden of proof lies clearly and heavily on the side of changing. Can the experiences related in paragraphs 2–5 bear that burden? The following responses will look into this question.

4. As indicated above, whenever one experiences an attraction that for one reason or another might be seen as from God, it is important to remember and try to be as precise as possible about the object of the drawing at the very time of experiencing it. What exactly was the person drawn to? Did the discerner add or subtract from the object of the drawing? This is clearly where Patrick failed. He had, without noticing that he was doing so, added to the drawing as it was experienced.

5. Again, rule II, 8, would help Patrick to understand the critical significance of his answer to the counselor's question. After the actual consolation he has added something to the attraction that came with it. Therefore, there is no reason to think that the conclusion he drew is from the Holy Spirit.

6. Patrick has been receiving genuine spiritual consolations (probably without previous cause) and with them attraction from the Holy Spirit to give himself more fully to God, to renounce all self-seeking. His response to this attraction has been generous but not wise. He has been led into the deception of unwittingly adding to the attraction from the Holy Spirit. There is no evidence to support this addition. The goals to which the Holy Spirit is drawing him can be achieved in a way of life that involves much active ministry, in a life of contemplation in action. Even the constant and strong desire for solitude is an inescapable part of such a life when it reaches some depth and fullness. Anyone who is called to be a contemplative in action and who forgoes the fulfillment of such desire for solitude in order to serve God experiences this as a sacrifice. The desire is especially strong when contemplation becomes passive, mystical, as seems to be happening with Patrick.

● *Response to Question for Case 24* ●

I would first ask Paul a series of questions: whether he was in a tranquil state when he did his deliberating (paragraph 2); whether he was truly indifferent to all but God's will; whether he was adequately informed about the new project, about its likely results, and about the consequences of his withdrawing from the other good work in which he was already involved; and whether his reasons all bore solely or primarily on the service and glory of God.

If these inquiries showed that Paul's discernment was not a sound one, I would explain to him that all the factors about which I had questioned him were of importance as he searched for God's will; and I would recommend that he give thought to all these factors before undertaking discernment again.

If after I had questioned him about these factors, it became clear that Paul had taken all of them into account, I would then explain to him the role played by his affective experiences (paragraph 3) as he sought to find God's will in what Ignatius names the second mode of election, making sure that he understood what constitutes a spiritual consolation and how the consolation and drawing should be related if the experience is to constitute evidence in the second mode of discernment. It seems clear from his account that the consolations were spiritual and prompted by the Holy Spirit. However, I would make sure of what he means by "frequently." Were the second-time experiences truly "plentiful," sufficient to justify a conclusion? If not, I would recommend prayer and waiting attentively to see whether God would give more evidence of this kind.

When Paul thinks he has done all that he reasonably can and has a sense that if he concludes and acts on his conclusion, he will be doing God's will, then it is time to make his decision. If at this time the evidence from the third mode of decision for the work he was already doing still appeared only slightly stronger, whereas in discernment by the second mode the evidence for the new work appeared to be very much stronger, I would recommend his tentatively choosing in accord with the evidence in the second mode.

I would then explain what is meant by "confirmation" of a decision and advise Paul to bring his tentative decision to God in prayer and beg for a confirmation or disconfirmation.

• *Response to Question for Case 25* •

I would again check Paul's dispositions and his information. I would discuss his reasons (paragraph 1) for a negative response to the governor, just to make sure they are as clear and strong as Paul thinks they are. If they are, then there is no need at all to consider the experience described in paragraph 2, for even if his second-time experience were such as could be prompted by the Holy Spirit, it would amount to nothing when weighed against the powerful evidence for the other alternative.

What is more, not only is the evidence supporting Paul's refusal of the governor's request overwhelmingly stronger, an affirmative response would be objectively sinful, a reneging on his clear moral responsibilities, as becomes clearer in paragraph 3. That being so, the affirmative alternative cannot be a valid one for Ignatian discernment of God's will. The latter is concerned only with alternatives already judged to be in themselves morally acceptable.

• *Response to the Question for Case 26* •

I would first help Paul to understand rule I, 13, apply it to his experience before he had come to talk with me, and commend him for escaping the trap set for him by the evil spirit.

I would then have Paul recall the essentials of spiritual consolation and spiritual desolation and see how these apply to the experiences he has narrated to me.

After that I would lead him to see how spiritual desolation, along with an inclination to question his earlier decision, came about as the result of a line of thought and feeling in continuity with the preceding spiritual consolation. Then I would go on to show how, by rules II, 3–5, the whole experience is to be judged as a deception by the evil spirit.

After that, we would consider how to respond to spiritual desolation (I, 6–9, 12).

Finally, using rule II, 7, I would give Paul advice on what his attitude should be in the future toward the experience of spiritual consolation. He should not let his recent experience of being deceived make him fidgety about spiritual consolation, immediately suspicious of it. Rather he should think that, until proved otherwise, genuine spiritual consolation is prompted by the Holy Spirit; he should be open to it as a gift of God, but be calmly alert for any sign of the evil spirit taking advantage of it. When he becomes aware of such a sign, he should immediately be on his guard and promptly oppose (I, 12) the line of thought and/or feeling that bears the mark of the evil spirit (II, 5).

• *Responses to Questions for Case 27* •

1. *a.* Leaving aside the series of "interior commands" that are preliminary to, not an intrinsic element of, the experience which came after she had carried them out, that experience corresponds with what Ignatius names consolation without previous cause (rules II, 2), more than with any other experience referred to in his rules. It is surely a spiritual consolation. There is in the event and in the consequent events no suggestion of its being prompted by any source other than the Holy Spirit. It seems to be effected by the Holy Spirit in Pauline immediately, without the mediation of any cognition or affection or volition that could serve as a ground for the consolation.

b. Neither the interior commands nor the consolation for which they were preparatory could provide Pauline with any evidence of God's calling her to one state of life rather than another. The essential factor in the constitution of second-time evidence for God's will is missing: there is no experience of being drawn to one or another alternative for choice during and integral with the consolation.

c. The *Suscipe* experience can be seen as a call to and a help to grow in love for God in preparation for receiving the later call to a state of life. Also, in reflection years afterwards (see paragraph 7), Pauline sees the interior command to go to her room and close the door as a symbolic indication (a "protograce") of the final step to which she would be called.

2. *a.* The third "touch" seems to correspond with Ignatius's description of the first time or occasion for a sound election. There is an experience of God's power, an unmistakable "message" regarding God's will for her, and an unshakable certainty about it. "I could not doubt the 'message' of the encounter, even if I wanted to," says Pauline.

b. The first two touches bear some incomplete resemblance to Ignatius's first-time for election but lack the unshakable certainty of God's directly moving her to what he showed to be his will. Pauline's ability so easily to brush the experiences away as meaningless demonstrates this lack. Within the context of the whole narrative, these incomplete experiences seem to have some providential significance, somehow leading up to the genuine first-time experience in the third of Pauline's touches.

c. In context and in common parlance among Catholics at that time, Pauline's exclamation "I have a vocation!" means a call to vows of poverty, celibacy, and obedience in community. It leaves open the question whether God is calling her to a cloistered contemplative community or to one that combines contemplation with active ministry to God's people. It also leaves open the further question of which community among either kind she is called to. These questions need to be answered by further discernments.

3. As we showed when treating the limits of discerning God's will, we cannot discern whether or not God intends us to actually do some act or achieve some goal. Discernment of God's will is not prophecy of future events. All we can find is what God wills us to intend efficaciously at the moment of finalizing the decision and thereafter until it becomes clear that God now wills us to intend something else efficaciously. Actual·achievement of what we intend in the future is not within the scope of discernment. Therefore, the development recounted in paragraph 8 could not confirm the truth of her conclusion any more than obstacles encountered in carrying it out could rightly be considered a disconfirmation, a sign that her conclusion was a mistaken one. The false assumption in either case would be that God always makes it easy to do his will. The happy event of which Pauline speaks can rightly be seen as assuring her that God is with her and, therefore, serves as a *volitional* confirmation, a strengthening of her will to carry out the decision she had already finalized.